RHODODENDRON

Reaktion's Botanical series is the first of its kind, integrating
horticultural and botanical writing with a broader account
of the cultural and social impact of trees, plants and flowers.

Rhododendron

Richard Milne

REAKTION BOOKS

To my beloved parents, Jane and Andrew

Published by
REAKTION BOOKS LTD
Unit 32, Waterside
44–48 Wharf Road
London N1 7UX, UK

www.reaktionbooks.co.uk

First published 2017
Copyright © Richard Milne 2017

Printed and bound in China by 1010 Printing International Ltd

A catalogue record for this book is available from the British Library

ISBN 978 1 78023 815 9

Contents

Rhododendron 'The General', a *catawbiense* hybrid.

Introduction:
Beauty and Bane

In the hills of western China grows a shrub that explodes into sheets of bright scarlet in late spring, earning it the name 'Yang Shan-hung', which means 'the whole mountain has turned to red' or 'mountain reflecting red'.[1] Horticulturalists would call it an azalea, whereas botanists would call it a *Rhododendron*, specifically *Rhododendron simsii*. The T'ang people, whose dynasty ruled China between AD 616 and 906, considered this flower to be the perfect symbol of their religion, and it is one of surprisingly few rhododendrons that have a long history in Chinese gardens.[2]

Rhododendrons including R. *simsii* also share another set of Chinese names, which are variants on 'goat staggers' or 'sheep staggering plant'.[3] There is no poetry to these names; they simply describe the partial paralysis suffered by livestock that unwisely eat the plant. Rhododendrons are poisonous, some more than others, and scattered reports of animal, and indeed human, poisonings come from anywhere they grow. Rhododendron poisoning was even once used as a weapon of mass slaughter. The rhododendron is something of a femme fatale, a beauty with a dark side.

Deciduous or evergreen, rhododendrons are versatile in form; some are compact and low, while a few reach the size of a tree. Their flowers can be as small as a button or as big as a hand, and may be any combination of white, yellow, pink, red and purple. In Europe and North America they are largely celebrated for their attractiveness as garden plants, although they have their detractors. Germaine Greer in her 'Rose Blight' persona called them 'appalling' and 'ghastly', lamenting:

> massed displays of rhododendron and azaleas, where the sweet variety of English gardening has been flung aside for mountainous injections of peat upon which these gross vegetable aliens may consent to live darkly, sucking light from the air to fuel their annual pyrotechnics.[4]

Many British folk think that they know two things about rhododendrons: they are invasive, and they come from the Himalayas. Both are half right: most of the hundreds grown in gardens do come from East Asia, but the only invasive species is *R. ponticum*, which hails from Europe and the Caucasus. Europe has very few native rhododendrons; among these the two alpenroses *R. ferrugineum* and *R. hirsutum* retain totemic status in their native Alps, but make poor garden plants.

Rhododendron simsii: 'mountain reflecting red' or 'sheep staggering plant' growing wild at Baili, Guizhou province, China.

Rhododendron ferrugineum (alpenrose) in a classic Alpine setting, in Austria.

North America, by contrast, has a few widespread evergreen species, but rather more deciduous 'azaleas'. The state of Washington made history in a way when it gave women the right to vote in 1892, in a one-off election that saw *R. macrophyllum* selected as the official state flower.[5] Men were excluded, and had to be content with electing politicians instead. Not to be outdone, West Virginia selected *R. maximum* for its own state flower in 1903, following a vote by schoolchildren.[6] The plant appears on the state flag, though you have to be told it is a rhododendron. The USA is one of numerous countries to have placed rhododendrons on its stamps – others include Germany (as early as 1938), Belarus, Myanmar, China, India, Nepal, Malaysia, the Marshall Islands, Poland and the USSR.

Unsurprisingly, rhododendrons are written far deeper into the culture of countries where people have lived alongside them for millennia. Chinese poems have been written about them for more than 1,000 years,[7] and folk tales abound, often linking them to departed souls and the cuckoo. There are flower festivals devoted to the plant, scenic areas named after them to attract tourists, and in one town the red-flowered *R. delavayi* is celebrated by illuminated street signs throughout the year.

Various rhododendron cultivars reflecting in the still pond at Isabella Plantation in London's Richmond Park. All are from the subgenus *Tsutsusi*, and most or all are derived from the Kurume azalea group.

Rhododendron arboreum is both the national flower of Nepal and the state flower of Uttarakhand in India. For local people there, however, rhododendrons are more significant for the everyday uses to which they are put, ranging from construction and firewood to food, pest control, incense and the treatment of an astonishing range of ailments.

The name *Rhododendron* means 'rose tree' in Greek. When in full bloom, the rhododendron is surely as beautiful as the rose, yet it cannot compare with it for cultural popularity. The rose is more manageable in size than most rhododendrons, and has a longer flowering season. However, the cultural dominance of the rose is probably down to it growing naturally throughout northern Europe, making it available to writers like Shakespeare long before the first ornamental rhododendron arrived. To many, roses simply *are* the flowers of love, taking pride of place in wedding bouquets. Even in parts of China where rhododendrons are everywhere, and steeped in romantic folklore, roses still manage to supplant them at weddings.

Thus when rhododendrons turn up in wedding bouquets or garlands, it is something of an innovation. The plants are much

Two rhododendron-themed stamps from the former USSR.
Left is *Rhododendron* 'zolotisti', a literal translation of *R. aureum*.

Street lights celebrate the cultural importance of *Rhododendron delavayi*,
in the Qianxi area of Bijie city, northwest Guizhou, China.

more likely to be present at the scene of a literary murder. Culturally
speaking, the perceived place for rhododendrons in Europe and the
United States is in large gardens and estates, golf courses and formal
plantings, even though in North America they also grow freely in the
hills. The Japanese had them in gardens probably before anyone else,
while the Chinese preferred to admire them in the wild.

When horticulture took off in Europe, intrepid collectors such
as Joseph Hooker, George Forrest and Frank Kingdon-Ward risked
everything to bring back new rhododendrons, and some died in
action. Equally important were the breeders, for no single species
was perfect for gardens, and the quest to combine perfect beauty and
form with full hardiness continues still.

Remarkably, *Rhododendron* is 60 million years old – older than the
Himalaya Mountains where most species grow. Through their long
history, rhododendrons have crossed oceans, advanced and retreated,
and exploded into the dizzying diversity that we see today. Natural

A wedding of two plant scientists in Yunnan, China. This region is steeped in rhododendron folklore, but roses still dominate the decorations, even for these two local plant scientists.

'Furnival's Daughter', one of the many thousands of named rhododendron cultivars created during the past 200 years.

hybridization has been important in the wild, as in gardens, and even helped make R. *ponticum* into a rampant invader.

This book, therefore, will examine the history of rhododendrons, both in the wild and in gardens, before examining their significance to mankind outside of gardens, especially in medicine and culture. The indomitable R. *ponticum* will get a chapter to itself, and the book will close with a look at the future for rhododendrons.

one

Sex and the Single Rhododendron

He crossed everything with rhododendrons except the chickens.
MRS CARL ENGLISH, speaking of Halfdan Lem (mid-20th century)

Last century, a French horticulturalist collected seeds from rhododendron plants in the Royal Botanic Garden, Edinburgh, in violation of garden rules. When the plants from the stolen seed flowered, they looked very different from the species that they had been taken from. Shamelessly, the horticulturalist wrote to the Royal Botanic Garden, telling them their plants were mislabelled. The letter caused some amusement, and was later used as an exam question, inviting students to explain what the Frenchman had so spectacularly overlooked.[1]

To pass, the students needed to understand that rhododendrons can and will cross naturally across species barriers, especially when related species grow side by side in gardens. The first known spontaneous hybrid was unveiled by William Thompson's nursery in 1819, an 'Azaleodendron' formed by natural cross-pollination in the garden between *R. calendulaceum* and *R. ponticum*.[2] That event inspired a frenzy of deliberate rhododendron hybrid creation, which continues to this day. Vital to this process has been that most rhododendron hybrids are highly fertile, allowing hybridization to continue through multiple generations, making it possible to breed out unwanted traits while combining desirable ones from two or more species. Hybrids are important in many other horticulturally significant genera, but

Rhododendron is exceptional, especially among woody plants, in the sheer numbers of wild and horticultural hybrids it produces.

A species is, more or less, a group of individuals that naturally breed with one another, and rarely or never outside the group. In practical terms, crossing any two individuals of the same species will give another similar plant, but crossing it with another gives a hybrid. Unlike species, hybrids do not come from true seed, meaning the offspring will look quite different to the parent individual, even if it is self-fertilized. For this reason, any rhododendron cultivar that is hybrid in origin will only keep its character if reproduced clonally, by cutting or layering. Hence when cultivar names are assigned to rhododendrons of hybrid origin, they normally apply uniquely to a single clone (exceptions to this tend to be very early hybrids). However,

One of the very few Azaleodendron hybrids, 'Glory of Littleworth'. Its exact parentage was known only to its breeder, but must have been a *Hymenanthes* (elepidote) rhododendron and a *Pentanthera* azalea.

named cultivars may also be selected forms within a species, and these often do come true from seed. Cultivars of this kind have the full species name followed by the cultivar name in quote marks: for example, *Rhododendron ponticum* 'variegatum'. These may or may not come true from seed, depending on the genetics of their defining traits, and of course who the father is.

Two other terms are worth knowing. A subspecies (ssp.) is a distinct and usually geographically separate form within a species; for example, *R. arboreum* has ssp. *arboreum* around Nepal and Sikkim, ssp. *delavayi* (or *R. delavayi*) in China, ssp. *nilagaricum* in southern India, and ssp. *zeylanicum* in Sri Lanka. The term 'variety' describes a less distinct form within a species, usually without geographical separation. For example, *R. wardii* var. *wardii* has yellow flowers, but in *R. wardii* var. *puralbum* they are white.[3] It is deeply regrettable that many commentators, including some who should really know better, sometimes use the terms 'species' and 'variety' interchangeably. Precise use of terms is never more important than when making sense of the bewildering diversity found in *Rhododendron*.

The purpose of flowers is to have sex, and the value of sex is that new combinations of genes are created with each generation. The sheer number of flowers a rhododendron produces, and the energy this must require, demonstrates how important sex is to them, especially given that they can reproduce without sex by layering. Look at

Rhododendron arboreum subspecies *arboreum* (left), *Rhododendron arboreum* ssp. *cinnamomeum* (middle), and *Rhododendron arboreum* ssp. *zeylanicum* (right). Three subspecies within the same species.

Rhododendron wardii var. *wardii* (left), and *Rhododendron wardii* var. *puralbum* (right). Natural varieties within the same species.

a newly opened rhododendron flower, and you may sometimes see strings of pollen hanging from its stamens. Vibration, such as from a buzzing bee, gentle wind or careful tapping, makes the stamens ejaculate their pollen; this forms into strings thanks to microscopic tentacles called viscin threads, and sticks to any insect that touches it.[4] The insect will then carry this to another flower, where the female pollen-receiving organ (stigma) provides a perfect landing pad.

Sex can make offspring that combine the strengths of each parent. It usually happens within a species, but interspecific crosses amplify these effects. *Rhododendron catawbiense* is frost hardy, while the tender *R. griffithianum* is far more beautiful. The best of their hybrids, 'Cynthia' and 'George Hardy', combined both traits, while those that did not were tossed aside by nurserymen. Natural selection works much the same way: those offspring with the best characters survive, allowing the species to evolve and adapt.

Watching bees dancing across a large rhododendron, one might detect a little problem. Much of the pollen gets transferred between different flowers on the same plant, which would lead to self-fertilization and hence inbreeding; it is of no help to the plant. To solve this problem, the female parts of *Rhododendron* flowers therefore favour pollen that comes from a different individual, thus ensuring wherever possible that each seed has a different father from its mother. This has been scientifically proved for *R. prinophyllum*.[5] A related but opposite mechanism in plants acts to favour pollen from the same species over that from different species, minimizing hybrid formation in the wild. Because of these two mechanisms, hybrids are most likely to form when pollen from a different individual of the same species is not available, such as when single individuals of different species grow together, as often happens in gardens or nurseries.

Rhododendrons hybridize freely, but there are limits. For a long time, it was believed that *Rhododendron* could hybridize with the barely related genus *Kalmia*,[6] producing two remarkable 'Kalmiodendron' cultivars. However, recent DNA evidence rejects this idea, suggesting instead that both Kalmiodendrons are in fact pure rhododendrons in which chance mutations have dramatically altered the flower shape.[7]

Gene combinations in hybrids can sometimes make them stronger in some ways than both their parents; for example, hybrids can have larger flowers than either parent, and *Rhododendron* 'Praecox' (*R. ciliatum* x *dauricum*) is hardier than *dauricum* or *ciliatum*.[8] This is termed 'hybrid

Left: strings of sticky pollen hanging from the anthers of *Rhododendron retivenium*, one of the tropical vireya group, in the montane tropics glasshouse at Edinburgh botanic gardens. Right: a pollinator lands on the style and stigma (female parts) of a flower of a *Rhododendron* hybrid ('Sarita Loder' x *calophytum*), delivering pollen in the process. The style provides an easier route to the nectar than scrambling on the petals.

F_1 hybrids 'Cynthia' (top left) and 'George Hardy' (top right). Both combine the showiness of parent *R. griffithianum* (bottom left) with hardiness from *R. catawbiense* (bottom right). The visible difference between the two hybrids can only result from genetic variation within the two parent species.

vigour'. First generation (F_1) hybrids contain one complete set of genes from each parent species, making them fairly consistent in form, as seen in wild populations of *R. ponticum* x *caucasicum*, or *ferrugineum* x *hirsutum*.[9] Differences between F_1s of a particular parentage reflect variation in the parent species; for example, 'George Hardy' is far paler than 'Cynthia', though both are *griffithianum* x *catawbiense*. Indeed, variation among *griersonianum* x *discolor* F_1s caused anger among buyers when the cultivar name 'Azor' was applied to any seed of such parentage, because they couldn't be sure what they were getting.[10]

During the 1840s the Waterer Nursery at Bagshot raised hundreds of F_1 seedlings from crosses between *arboreum* and *maximum*, but among them one particular individual outshone all the others and had the potential to make them a fortune. Its dowdier sisters were sold in bulk for a landscape planting in Maidenhead, but the horrified foreman then realized too late that he had failed to specify that one particular plant should certainly *not* be taken. Nurserymen would later tell of

'Everlasting', a supposed 'Kalmiodendron' hybrid between *Rhododendron williamsianum* and the mountain laurel *Kalmia latifolia*, is indicated by DNA to be a pure *Rhododendron*. It is probably a mutant *Rhododendron* with abnormal flower shape, possibly of *R. brachycarpum* or another member of the Pontica group.

how he embarked on a desperate rescue mission, sneaking into the Maidenhead property under the cover of night, where he located the prize specimen and replaced it with a much less precious sister plant.[11] The rescued plant became the celebrated 'Lady Eleanor Cathcart'. Between-F_1 variation can, therefore, make the difference between a money-spinning prize cultivar and an also-ran.

A wise hybridizer will turn within-species variation to his advantage. After Sir Edmund Loder inherited the Leonardslee estate in 1889, he chose the largest- and sweetest-flowered *R. fortunei* in his garden, and requested from his neighbour pollen of an especially fine plant of *R. griffithianum*. This produced the Loderi group, a series of sister F_1s whose scented flowers are among the largest on any rhododendron, or indeed any cultivated shrub that grows outdoors in Britain. Even so, the F_1s raised were not identical to one another, because like any group of full siblings, they received varying genetic information from each parent individual. For example, some are white flowered, and others pink.[12]

Between-hybrid variation is far greater in hybrid generations following the F_1, because any offspring from an F_1 inherits some, but not all, of the genes from each parent species, and it will be different genes in every case. Hence some genes will be missing, sometimes with dramatic effects; for example, double or 'hose-in-hose' flowers are caused by the absence of a gene that regulates flower development, turning stamens or sepals into extra petals, as in the Kurume azaleas

Rhododendron 'Praecox' (top), a hardy F_1 hybrid between the moderately hardy *R. dauricum* (bottom left) and the tender *R. ciliatum* (bottom right, note frost damage to flowers).

Loderis: six named progeny of a cross between two carefully chosen individual plants, showing subtle variation, as occurs between any full siblings. Top (l–r) 'Loderi White Diamond', 'Loderi Venus', 'Loderi Pink Topaz'; bottom (l–r) 'Loderi Game Chick', 'Loderi King George', 'Loderi Patience'.

discussed below, and the vireya Balsamaeflorum group described in Chapter Four. This genetic lottery creates massive variation among second and later generation hybrids; scientists call this segregation.

In Baili, western China, a massive population of hybrids between the creamy white-flowered R. *irroratum* and the red R. *delavayi* contains flowers of every shade in between; the colour may even vary within one plant. Armies of tourists are bussed around in specially constructed little carts to the best spots to witness the spectacle. Then for the rest of the year the hotels largely stand empty and the carts unused; even the brilliant red flowers of R. *simsii* that come a few weeks later pass largely unseen.

In fact, the effects of segregation can be seen and admired in our gardens, thanks to one of the most celebrated groups of rhododendron cultivars. The great plant collector Ernest Wilson came to the town of Kurume, Japan in 1918, where he found nursery after nursery stacked full of hundreds of rhododendron cultivars. These became

opposite: 'Lady Eleanor Cathcart', by far the best of a large progeny of *Rhododendron maximum* x *arboreum* F₁ siblings raised by the Waterer nursery at Bagshot.

known as the Kurume azaleas; Wilson called them 'the loveliest of all azaleas'. The flowers could be anything from white to scarlet red, and varied greatly in shape and size. Some had sepals converted into an extra whorl of petals ('hose-in-hose'). He was told that most of them descended from a single plant of cultivar 'Azuma-Kagami', which in turn had been collected from Mount Kirishima. The mountain is a sacred site in Japan, for in legend it was the landing site of Ninigi-no-Mikoto, grandson of Amaterasu the sun goddess, and supposed ancestor of the Japanese imperial line.[13] Wilson exported fifty of the best cultivars to Europe and North America, most of which survive in cultivation today. However, his request to purchase the original 'Azuma-Kagami' plant for export was politely refused.[14]

We now know that the Mount Kirishima population comprises hybrids between *R. kiusianum* and *R. kaempferi*.[15] The incredible range of forms produced here, and preserved as cultivars, probably explains why early botanist Kaempfer identified 21 different kinds of Japanese azalea, whereas Thunberg thought these were all one supervariable species. All of the forms present among the Kurume azalea cultivars occur among this wild hybrid population, indicating that their diversity results from segregation of variation from just these two species.[16]

Parents of the Kurume azaleas. Left: 'Azuma Kagami', the hybrid cultivar from which all pink Kurume azaleas are reportedly descended. Right: the parent species *R. kiuisanum* (top) and *R. kaempferi* (bottom).

Why, when so many hybrids are produced, do R. *kiusianum* and R. *kaempferi* not simply merge into one confused great mass? Why are wild hybrids normally the exception, and not the rule? As noted above, flowers have the ability to favour pollen of their own species when it is available, which keeps F_1 formation to a minimum, but once an F_1 is formed, it can potentially sire a large dynasty of hybrids, as at Baili and Kirishima. The key may lie in ecology: R. *kiusianum* is a high-altitude species with small, deciduous leaves, whereas R. *kaempferi* is a low-altitude species with larger evergreen leaves. Within its natural altitude range, each species is favoured by natural selection over hybrids, and it is only in the narrow belt between them that hybrids can prosper.

Also occupying a narrow altitudinal belt is R. x *sochadzeae*, which grows at around 1,900 m (6,230 ft) on mountain slopes looking north towards the Black Sea in northeast Turkey. Its parents R. *ponticum* and R. *caucasicum* grow below and above it, respectively. Remarkably, all the hybrid plants seem to be first generation; perhaps having one complete set of genes from each parent species makes them perfectly equipped to live halfway up the mountain slope.[17] Similarly, in the Alps of Austria, R. *ferrugineum* occurs on acid soils, R. *hirsutum* on base-rich soils, and their hybrid R. x *intermedium* forms large patches of mainly first generation hybrids where pH is intermediate.[18]

Segregation produces variation in ecological needs as well as appearance. Hence when human beings disturb the landscape and create unfamiliar habitats, second-generation hybrids often tend to do rather well. Both Baili and Kirishima have been altered by centuries of intensive human activity; northeast Turkish mountains and the Alps less so. Even outside of gardens, humans have inadvertently been promoting the production of new hybrid forms in *Rhododendron*.

Later chapters will focus more on hybrids that have been deliberately created, but Kurume azaleas are remarkable in that they replicate in our gardens the kind of variation that hybridization generates in the wild. Many of them can be seen at the Punch Bowl at Windsor Great Park, a stunning setting overlooking Virginia Water,

Kurume azaleas: twenty of 'Wilson's Fifty' cultivars imported from Japan.
Top to bottom and left to right: Aioi, Asa-Gasumi, Aya Kammuri, Benifude,
Bijinsui, Hachika Tsugi, Hana-Asobi, Hinode Giri, Hinode no Taka, Ho o,
Ima Shojo, Iro Hayama, Kasane Kagaribi, Kasume-Gaseki, Katsura no Hana,
Kimigayo, Kirin, Kiritsubo, Kumo no Uye, Kurai no Himo.

Kurume azaleas continued: twenty more of 'Wilson's Fifty' cultivars imported from Japan. Top to bottom and left to right: Kureno Yuki, Odome (Otome), Oino Mezame and Omoine; Osaraku Seedling, Rasho Mon, Saotome, Seikai; Shin Seikai, Shin Utena, Shintoki no Hagasane, Suga No Ito; Sui Yohi, Takasogo, Tama no Utena, Tancho; Tsuta Momji, Ukamuse (identification not certain), Waka Kayede, Yoro Zuyo.

A stream running through Isabella Plantation in London's Richmond Park, with plantings of numerous different *Tsutsusi* hybrid cultivars along either side.

The Punch Bowl in the Valley Garden above Virginia Water, showcasing Kurume azaleas.

or Isabella Plantation in London's Richmond Park (both free to enter). Elsewhere, the Kurume azaleas have to some extent been supplanted by modern hybrids bred from them but involving additional species, such as 'Malvatica' and its progeny.

two

The Fall and Rise of *Azalea*

※

To tell them apart, first look at a flower – *most* azaleas have only
5 or 6 stamens, while *most* rhododendrons have 10 stamens.
'AZALEAS', www.azaleas.org, 14 July 2007

I
n around 1995 *Rhododendron* expert David Chamberlain was called upon to act as an expert witness in an acrimonious dispute between neighbours, one of whom wanted to bulldoze the line of shrubs separating their properties. The other cited a strict stipulation that had been placed on both properties, that the rhododendron plants separating them were not to be removed. But, said the first, these were not rhododendrons, they were azaleas, so the stipulation didn't apply![1]

Certainly, there are few more familiar plant names than 'azalea'. The website www.rhododendrons.com lists more than 1,000 azalea cultivars, whereas www.azaleas.org asserts that 10,000 kinds exist in total. Scientifically speaking, however, azaleas do not exist. They are all *Rhododendron*, and some 'azaleas' are not even closely related to certain others. Hence the 'azaleas' separating the warring neighbours' properties were reprieved, and a grudging compromise involving their husbandry was reached.[2] Yet how did the tangled botanical naming that precipitated this dispute come about?

The first recorded attempt at systematic classification of rhododendrons was in 1495, when a Chinese text recognized twenty kinds of rhododendron.[3] In the West, however, species came to the attention of science one by one. In 1680 a plant known as '*Chamaerhododendron*

The six original members of the now defunct genus *Azalea* as described by Linnaeus:
A. procumbens (now *Kalmia procumbens*), *A. nudiflorum* (now *R. periclymenoides*), *A. pontica*
(now *R. luteum*), *A. viscosum*, *A. lapponica* and *A. indica*.

exoticum amplissimus floribus liliaceis frutex spectabilis elegans' was described
from cultivation in Holland,[4] having made its way from Japan, probably via Java. Meanwhile in Virginia, the English missionary John
Bannister had been sending sketches of American plants to the great
botanist John Ray, and among them was '*Cistus Virginiana, flore & odore
Periclymeni*'. Another American plant, '*Cistus virginiana Periclymeni flore
ampliore minus odorato*', soon followed. To these were added a European
alpine species, in 1737: '*Azalea ramis diffuso procumbentibus*'.[5]

Botanical naming was, evidently, cumbersome and unsystematic.
This was changed in 1753 by the genius of Linnaeus, who renamed
these four plants, respectively, as *Azalea indica*, *A. viscosa*, *A. lutea* (now *R.
periclymenoides*[6]) and *A. procumbens*, and added *A. pontica* (now *R. luteum*)
and *A. lapponica*. Even at this early stage, the azaleas were a mixture of
the evergreen (*indica*, *lapponica* and *procumbens*) and deciduous.

Linnaeus's great insight was to classify plants according to the
number and arrangement of their floral parts. His six *Azalea*s all had
five stamens and five fused petals, and this separated them, for example, from *Cistus*, which has numerous stamens and unjoined petals.

However, Linnaeus also had specimens of five more species that resembled *Azalea*, but had ten stamens. They could not, under his system, be the same genus as five-stamened *Azalea*, so he called them *Rhododendron*. These five species were *R. maximum* from North America, *R. dauricum* from Siberia, and three alpine species, *R. chamaecistus*, *R. ferrugineum* and *R. hirsutum*. *Rhododendron ponticum* would soon follow. Thus was born a schism that, in the horticultural world at least, would endure forever.

Following similar principles, two more genera would later be erected with ten stamens but different numbers of petals: Linnaeus in 1762 described the deciduous *Rhodora* from Canada and nearby, with apparently just three petals (one is in fact three petals fused together), whereas in 1826 Karl Ludwig Blume erected the evergreen *Hymenanthes* from Japan, with seven petals. In the same year, Blume also created a fifth genus, *Vireya*, for *V. malayana*, a delicate tropical plant.

The genus *Azalea* slowly grew in size after 1753, via the discovery of occasional new *Pentanthera* group species from North America, such

The five original members of the genus *Rhododendron* as described by Linnaeus: *R. hirsutum*, *R. chamaecistus* (now *Rhodothamnus chamaecistus*), *R. maximum*, *R. dauricum*, *R. ferrugineum*.

Rhododendrons that were put in separate genera for a while: *R. canadensis* (*Rhodora*), *R. degronianum heptamerum* (*Hymenanthes japonicum*) and *R. malayanum* (*Vireya*).

as *R. calendulaceum* and *R. canescens*, described by Michaux in 1803. By this time, however, there were the first grumblings of discord, with Salisbury in 1796 first suggesting that *Rhododendron* and *Azalea* should be merged.[7] In 1824 four *Azalea* species were transferred to *Rhododendron*, and by 1834 all remaining *Azalea* species, including recent additions *A. molle*, *A. arborescens* and *A. mucronatum*, were likewise transferred.[8] Not everyone agreed with this, however.

Evergreen azaleas allied to *R. indicum* then began arriving from China and Japan. By 1863 there were ten of these,[9] but some had ten stamens and others had five, making Linnaeus's distinction for *Azalea* look increasingly shaky. The discovery of *R. schlippenbachii* in

Kamchatka and R. *albrechtii* in Korea further demonstrated that
species with ten stamens could be deciduous, while R. *degronianum*
from Japan was nearly identical to *Hymenanthes japonicum* except for
having five petals. In 1876 the rare American R. *vaseyi* was discovered, which resembled *Rhodora canadensis* but had seven stamens and
five petals.[10] Simple dividing lines among these plants could not
logically be maintained.

Taxonomy is an odd science, proceeding as it does by opinion,
disagreement and consensus. Just because one scientist erects a new
species, or transfers a species to a new genus, does not mean that

Rhododendrons that challenged the separation of *Azalea, Rhodora* and *Hymenanthes*:
R. *degronianum* (clearly *Hymenanthes*, but with five petals not seven), R. *schlippenbachii*
(deciduous with ten stamens), R. *vaseyi* (like *Rhodora* but five petals and five or
seven stamens), R. *rubropilosum* (*Tsutsusi*, five stamens) and R. *yedoense poukhanense*
(*Tsutsusi*, ten stamens).

Rhododendron semibarbatum: an anomalous *Rhododendron* species placed on its own in subgenus *Mumeazelea*. Recent molecular data suggest it might be closer to *R. nipponicum* than to any other species.

anyone else is obliged to accept it. This may seem quaintly inefficient, but it acts as a vital check against misguided and unhelpful decisions, such as renaming the British *R. ponticum* populations as *R.* x *superponticum*.[11]

Therefore, botanists were free to disagree about merging *Azalea* with *Rhododendron*, and several did. None of the evergreen azaleas, nor the deciduous ten-stamened species, occur in North America, so for those who focused on the native flora there, the distinction remained simple: deciduous = *Azalea*, evergreen = *Rhododendron*. Hence between 1824 and 1943 there occurred a sort of botanical tug-of-love. New deciduous or five-stamened species that were initially described as *Azalea* were swiftly transferred by other authors into *Rhododendron*, and vice versa. For example, three new American *Azalea* species were added by Small in 1913, then moved to *Rhododendron* by Rehder in 1917. Small retaliated by transferring Rehder's *R. alabamense* into *Azalea* in 1933, but he was swimming against the tide. The very last attempted addition to *Azalea* was the transfer of *R. cumberlandense* to *Azalea* by Copeland in 1943, which others ignored.[12] From this point onwards *Azalea* as a distinct genus, or a scientific entity, ceased to exist.

By the early twentieth century, *Rhododendron* was becoming a bloated monster, for even as it gobbled up *Azalea*, *Rhodora*, *Vireya* and *Hymenanthes*, it was rapidly swelling thanks to legions of new species being discovered in Asia – a process that would eventually bring its species count above 1,000. To make sense of this diversity, a sensible system of subdivision was needed, so *Rhododendron* is now divided into eight subgenera.[13] Subgenus *Rhododendron*, which includes the tropical vireyas, has 462 species, termed 'lepidote rhododendrons' due to scales under their leaves. Next largest is subgenus *Hymenanthes*, containing 224 'elepidote' (that is, without scales) evergreen species, followed by *Tsutsusi* comprising eighty evergreen to deciduous 'azaleas'. Subgenera *Pentanthera* and *Azaleastrum* contain eighteen and sixteen 'azalea' species respectively, with *Pentanthera* containing most of the North American *Rhododendron* species. Finally, subgenera *Candidastrum*, *Mumeazalea* and *Therorhodion* contain one species each (though a second *Therorhodion* is sometimes recognized). The larger subgenera are further subdivided into sections and subsections.

More recently, DNA evidence has revealed the actual evolutionary relationships between the species of *Rhododendron*, supporting some of these groupings and challenging others. First, various DNA studies concur that *Azalea* and *Rhododendron* are certainly not distinct.[14] They confirm that each of subgenera *Rhododendron*, *Hymenanthes* and *Tsutsusi* are natural groups, or 'monophyletic' in scientific parlance. That is, all members of each group descend from a common ancestor, from which no species outside the group are descended. Conversely, *Azaleastrum* contains two unrelated evolutionary lines. Likewise, the North American *Pentanthera* species, plus R. *luteum* and R. *molle*, are closer to the evergreen subgenus *Hymenanthes* than to other azaleas previously placed in *Pentanthera*. Indeed, the existence of 'Azaleodendron' crosses between these subgenera, such as 'Glory of Littleworth', testifies to their closeness, as otherwise hybrids between *Rhododendron* subgenera are extremely hard or impossible to produce.

Most dramatically, this DNA evidence has strongly indicated that the genera *Ledum* and *Menziesia*, which do not look at all like rhododendrons, nonetheless belong in the genus. The egg-shaped flowers of *Menziesia* look more like the genus *Erica* than a *Rhododendron*, but this probably reflects strong natural selection for a different flower shape. Its closest relatives seem to include R. *albiflorum*, R. *schlippenbachii* and R. *vaseyi*. When further DNA evidence clarifies its relationships, *Menziesia* is likely to be reclassified as subgenus *Menziesia* within *Rhododendron*. *Ledum* is already reduced to section *Ledum* within subgenus *Rhododendron*.

All of the eight original *Rhododendron* subgenus names derive from genera that were originally described as distinct, like *Hymenanthes*, and then merged into *Rhododendron*. This begs the question: why is *Azalea* not among them? In botanical classification, when a new genus is erected, the genus name is attached to one species in particular, known as the type. Should the genus later be split into two, the group that includes the type will retain the original name, while the other group is given a new name.

The type species of *Rhododendron* is the alpenrose R. *ferrugineum*, while that for *Azalea* was A. *procumbens*. By unhappy chance, this was the only *Azalea* never to be transferred into *Rhododendron*, because it differs in important characteristics like leaf arrangement. Indeed, it was put into a separate genus from the other azaleas in 1813. Under normal rules the name *Azalea* would have gone with it, but to avoid confusion the new genus was given a new name, *Loiseleuria*. Hence the other

Menziesia ciliicalyx may not look much like a rhododendron, but DNA evidence clearly shows that it is in fact a highly modified member of the genus *Rhododendron*.

azaleas remained in *Azalea*, to the relief of gardeners, but the genus *Azalea* now lacked a type species, meaning the name could not be used for a subgroup when it was subsumed into *Rhododendron*.[15] DNA evidence now indicates that *Loiseleuria procumbens* properly belongs in *Kalmia*.[16]

Even as they were disappearing from scientific texts, azaleas were multiplying at an exponential rate in gardens. Almost all of the horticultural hybrids that started appearing in large numbers in the nineteenth century were either azaleas involving subgenus *Pentanthera* species, or rhododendrons involving either subgenus *Hymenanthes* or (less often) subgenus *Rhododendron*. Because subgenera almost never cross, each subgenus has a separate and distinct history of cultivar development. The story of *Pentanthera* azalea cultivars (at least in Europe) began in earnest with the Ghent azaleas.

Azaleas have one clear advantage over evergreen rhododendrons, especially for the experimental hybridizer and nurseryman: they reach flowering age more quickly, as little as two years after germination.[17] Hence azalea hybrids began to appear more quickly in gardens than

Ghent azaleas. Top (l–r): 'Gloria Mundi', 'Nancy Waterer', 'Irene Koster'; middle (l–r): 'Unique', 'Norma', 'Daviesii'; bottom (l–r): 'Corneille', 'Narcissiflorum', 'Pucella'.

rhododendrons. While the English might have been first to start hybridizing these, they were eclipsed by the work of one P. Mortier, a baker by trade, from Belgium. He produced a whole set of cultivars, which came to be known as the Ghent azaleas. These were bred from five *Pentanthera* species: *R. luteum*, *R. calendulaceum* and *R. periclymenoides* (then called *A. nudiflorum*), and less often *R. viscosum* and *R. arborescens*. They arrived in Britain in the 1830s, to great acclaim, and in 1836 no fewer than 72 kinds were listed in a single catalogue, rising later to over 200. They were lauded for their colour range, fragrance and hardiness.[18] The Victorian gardener Henry Bright, however, observed a darker side:

It is generally known that no fly-catcher is more cruel and more greedy than the common Ghent Azalea, especially, I think, the sweet yellow one? On one single blossom . . . I found no less than six flies, four of them quite dead, and of one or two nothing remained but a shred of wing. Two others were still alive, but the Azalea had nearly drained their life away, and held them so tightly in its viscid hairs that I could hardly release them from its grasp . . . the entire Azalea shrub had probably caught some hundreds.[19]

The name 'Ghent Azaleas' derives from where Mortier worked, but originally could be applied to any hybrid derived from the five stated species and no others, wherever bred; for example, 'Nancy Waterer' from Knaphill in Surrey. Recently, Ghent azaleas have earned the distinction of being the first ornamental plant of any kind to gain PGI (Protected Geographical Indication) status, making them the botanical equivalent of the Arbroath Smokie, Cornish Pasty or Roquefort cheese.[20] Among newly bred cultivars, only those raised in and around Ghent in the East Flanders region of Belgium may claim the name of Ghent azalea.

Ghent azaleas shone brilliantly among the gardening world at first, but many have now vanished from cultivation.[21] They soon began to face increasing competition as new introductions sired new generations of hybrids. *Rhododendron molle*, originally called *Azalea mollis*, comprises the normally yellow subspecies *molle* of China, and subspecies *japonicum* from Japan, which varies from yellow through orange to bright red. Cultivars whose ancestry involves this species, Ghent azaleas and/or their parent species, are collectively termed the Mollis Azalea group, known for their showy, mainly red and orange flowers. These were produced independently by two Belgians: Louis van Houtte before 1870, and later the Koster family from 1892 onwards. By 1877 there were masses of Ghent and Mollis Azaleas in Belgium, but they had not yet become common in British gardens.[22]

British nurserymen were far from idle during this period. Particularly significant in the azalea story is Knap Hill near Bagshot, Surrey, which first became a rhododendron nursery after 1770, when Michael Waterer acquired and drained a bog. In time the property and business passed to his son Michael Junior, but when he died in 1842, the business was split between his two brothers. Hosea retained the Knap Hill property, while John inherited the recently acquired Bagshot Nursery, beginning a rivalry that persisted until the Great War. Hosea publicized the Knap Hill Nursery by sending large numbers of rhododendrons and azaleas to London via distinctive horse carts and by train. Next to inherit was his nephew Anthony, initially in partnership with Robert Godfrey. From 1870 to 1890 Anthony would exhibit his

Mollis azaleas. Top (l–r): 'Koster's Brilliant Red' and 'Anthony Koster', 'Brilliant Red'; middle (l–r): 'Spek's Orange', 'Snowdrift', 'Christopher Wren'; bottom (l–r): 'Spek's Brilliant', 'Lemonara', 'Dr M. Oosthoek'.

Knap Hill azaleas raised by the Waterer family. Top (l–r): 'Gog', 'Whitethroat';
bottom (l–r): 'Double Damask', 'Golden Oriole'.

rhododendrons and azaleas in London's Regent's Park while his cousin and rival John Junior did the same in nearby Cadogan Place.[23]

Anthony Waterer was an eccentric character, who banned frost-sensitive plants from his nursery after a harsh winter slaughtered thousands of *Araucaria imbricaria* seedlings.[24] However, he saw the potential in *R. occidentale*, which was introduced to Britain by William Lobb in 1851, and marketed by Veitch Nurseries. To many, this was just another pale azalea, none too different from *R. periclymenoides*.[25] Anthony, however, noted a fine scent, larger, well-presented flowers, interesting foliage with good autumn colours, and relatively late blooming, even past midsummer, which avoided damage from frost. Through hybridization, Anthony combined these useful traits with the best of the Mollis and Ghent azaleas, creating the Knap Hill Azalea group.

Initially, however, these azaleas offered little competition to the Ghent or Mollis groups, for the simple reason that Anthony Junior,

Exbury azaleas. Top (l–r): 'Basilisk', 'Clarice', 'Exbury White';
bottom (l–r): 'Gibraltar', 'Pink Delight', 'Sunte Nectarine'.

who inherited the business in 1896, was generally unwilling to part with them. He never married, and was an autocratic character, rich enough to afford a few eccentricities.[26] Like a reclusive artist, he preferred to keep his finest creations to himself, and on occasion would suddenly order the destruction of a batch that he decided was not up to scratch. Also, *Pentanthera* hybrids are more difficult to propagate asexually than evergreen rhododendrons,[27] and like all hybrids do not come true from seed, which might have further discouraged selling them in large numbers. As a result, the Knap Hill hybrids did not appear in public catalogues until after he died. His cousin Gomer (son of John) then took over the site and rescued as many plants there as he could. Gomer's son Donald was the last male of the Waterer line, and bred many fine hybrids from Anthony's plants.[28]

One man who did persuade Waterer to part with a set of the Knap Hill Azaleas was Lionel de Rothschild.[29] Soon after acquiring the Exbury estate in Hampshire, in 1919, Rothschild set about crossing these azaleas with vigour and passion, hoping to improve their colour. After two generations, he began exhibiting the best plants, including during an acclaimed appearance at the Chelsea Flower

Show. Suddenly the Exbury azaleas, as they were known, became the plants to have, basking in limelight denied to their progenitors the Knap Hills.[30] Demand from the public was far too great to be met by vegetative propagation, even with the vast operation Rothschild had built up on his ample land. Therefore, they were reproduced by seed, grown up and sold in groups according to flower colour, which worked fine if buyers could see the flowering plants. However, when sold as seed (as they had to be to North America, for example), the buyer could not be sure what they were getting, as hybrids do not come true from seed (see Chapter One).[31] If the seller was upfront about this then fair enough, but some led buyers to believe that their seed would replicate the female parent,[32] leading to angry responses:

> The naming of entire batches of hybrid seedlings with the same clonal name . . . has proven to be an abomination here in the United States where many of these never alike seed-lings are being grown under the same name.[33]

From the Exbury Azaleas were bred several further groups, each defined more by history or location than any particular characters, because after the Knap Hills no new characters of significance had been introduced from adding parent species. These new groups include the Solent group developed by Lionel's son, and the Ilam group from New Zealand. The Windsor group were bred by Eric Savill from plants gifted to royal rhododendron enthusiasts King George VI and his wife Queen Elizabeth, and are showcased in the Savill Gardens in Windsor Great Park. Inevitably, countless cultivars have been lost, especially older ones.[34] However, some survive from every wave of production, including a few like 'Gloria Mundi' from the 1836 catalogue containing original Ghents.[35] Kew and the Sir Harold Hiller Gardens have excellent collections. Meanwhile, enthu-siasts all over the place are busily creating new ones. In our gardens, if not in our textbooks, azalea lives.

three
Rhododendromania

🙟

[*Rhododendron catawbiense*] is perhaps the most valuable evergreen
shrub for ornament ever introduced. In the hands of nurserymen,
but chiefly of the Waterers, it has given birth by hybridisation
to the most valuable group of rhododendrons in existence – the
group which flowers at the end of May and in June.

WILLIAM BEAN, *Trees and Shrubs Hardy in the British Isles* (1916)

B y around 1810 about nineteen rhododendrons had been
brought into cultivation in Europe, including eight American
species, five from Europe and the Caucasus, four from Russia
and northeast Asia, and *R. indicum* from Japan. Besides the azaleas, discussed in Chapter Two, there were the two alpine species, *ferrugineum*
and *hirsutum*, neither of which has ever done particularly well in gardens.
There was *R. ponticum* and, recently arrived, the barely distinguishable
R. catawbiense, plus their relative *R. maximum* ('the best that can be
said of it is that it means well', to paraphrase Street[1]). The delicate *R.
dauricum* was available, along with *R. aureum*, *R. caucasicum*, *R. fragrans* and
R. minus, but though many were hardy, none had particular beauty.[2]
Therefore, even through hybridization there was little that could be
achieved from this raw material, certainly nothing to rival the glory
of the Ghent azaleas. All this would be changed, dramatically, by the
arrival from India of seeds packed in a tin of brown sugar.

To set the scene, the British East India Company was founded
on the very last day of the sixteenth century, and a Dutch equivalent

Rhododendron arboreum,
the first rhododendron
to be introduced from
India, via seeds packed in
sugar. Painting from J. S.
Kerner's *Hortus sempervirens*
(1792).

quickly followed. After this, permanent trading posts began appearing around the Indian coast, and the communities that built up around them needed medical men. Many of these were amateur botanists, and took advantage of their station to discover and, where possible, export exotic plants.

Nathaniel Wallich was a Danish man who, aged just 21, took up the post of surgeon at Serampore in West Bengal, near Calcutta (Kolkata).[3] It was 1807, and his timing was unfortunate, for Britain would soon attack Copenhagen, dragging Denmark into the Napoleonic wars. Serampore was occupied, and Wallich ended 1808 as a prisoner of war. He was rescued by a request for an assistant from the ageing William Roxburgh, surgeon of the British East India Company in Calcutta, and director of its botanic garden.[4]

Wallich assisted Roxburgh for three years from 1809, then gradually took over running the garden as his mentor took ill, although not without a battle, for again his nationality counted against him.[5]

A large plant of *Rhododendron arboreum* at Kew.

Roxburgh pined for his native Scottish flora, but Wallich took to Indian plants with a passion. However, the interior of India was hard to reach, due to barriers both geographic and political. Hence Wallich eagerly received seeds and specimens sent from Kathmandu by Edward Gardner, the British Resident there. Among them was the recently described *R. arboreum*. Despite having never seen a live plant of it, Wallich sent some of Gardner's seeds to Britain in 1814, packed in sugar, which neatly protected them from mould.[6]

Rhododendron arboreum is tall, stately and has deep pink to red flowers, so it easily outshone any evergreen rhododendron introduced to Europe so far, but it was far from hardy. This drawback became a massive stimulus, however, for here was the perfect problem to be solved by the emerging art of rhododendron hybridization.

Crossed with the dowdy *R. maximum*, it gave 'Lady Eleanor Cathcart', the beauty that the Waterer Nursery had to rescue from Maidenhead (see Chapter One). With the dwarf alpine *R. caucasicum* it bred 'Nobleanum', and with the super-hardy *catawbiense*, 'John Walter'. Crossed with a *catawbiense* x *ponticum* hybrid, it sired the stately 'Alta-clarense' (the name being a Latinization of Highclere where it was bred – and where *Downton Abbey* was filmed). All combined the bright colour of *arboreum* with the hardiness of other species, setting the mould for all rhododendron breeding that was to follow.

For Wallich, the twenty years from 1815 must have been a golden era of joy and discovery. He visited Nepal, Singapore, Sumatra, Java and Burma (now Myanmar), but often his opportunities to botanize were limited, and he relied greatly on seed and specimens sent to him.

Early *Rhododendron* hybrids. Left: 'Altaclarense' ((*catawbiense* x *ponticum*) x *arboreum*, 1826). Right (top to bottom): 'Nobleanum' (*caucasicum* x *arboreum*, 1832); 'Broughtonii' (*arboreum* x unknown, 1840); 'Caucasicum pictum' (*caucasicum* x unknown, 1853).

He was involved in the introduction of five more rhododendrons: *aeruginosum, anthopogon, setosum, formosum* and most significantly *R. campanulatum*, which gave rise to the hardy 'Bodartianum' and other fine cultivars like 'Waxen Bell'. Meanwhile he passionately built up the living collections of the Calcutta garden, prompting the locals to call it 'Wallich's Pet'.[7] Then in 1835 a man arrived who would disrupt Wallich's world.

Born in 1810, William Griffith was a botanist of exceptional talent and keenness, who came to Madras as an assistant surgeon in 1832.[8] Unlike Wallich, his post gave him ample spare time in which to botanize, and he must have been delighted when he was offered the chance to join a botanical expedition to Assam.[9]

Assam had recently been ceded to the British by Burma following the Burmese war. The war had been crippling for both countries, and the financial cost caused the East India Company to lose its monopoly on trade with China.[10] It needed a new source of tea, and a report from the Scottish adventurer Robert Bruce that tea plants grew wild in Assam provided the perfect solution.[11] Hence they sent Wallich,

Rhododendron campanulatum 'Waxen bell'.

Feuding botanists: William Griffith (1810–1845) and Nathaniel Wallich (1786–1854).

Griffith and the geologist John McClelland to go and investigate the possibility of establishing a British tea industry in Assam.[12]

After many weeks struggling through the Ganges basin, the trio were able to spend a month exploring the botanical hotspot of Cherrapunji, which must have been a dream come true for Griffith. He wanted to collect and press everything he saw, but he could not, because they had not brought enough flower press material. Wallich was methodical and selective in which species he gathered, and had packed accordingly. Having patiently learned the methods of botany from Roxburgh, he probably expected the younger Griffith to defer to his judgement, and his methods. Griffith, however, was a raw talent who seems to have felt no need to take advice. Wallich probably told Griffith to collect fewer plants, but Griffith might have countered that it was not his fault they had too few flower presses. Eventually, a furious Griffith caught Wallich removing some of Griffith's specimens from the flower press.[13]

Arriving in Assam with such animosity, the two men predictably had opposing opinions on how to set up a tea industry there. Griffith and McClelland suggested growing native tea, but Wallich was adamant that imported Chinese varieties should be grown. Desperate

'Wallich's Pet': an old postcard of the garden at Calcutta.

to get away from both Griffith and Assam, Wallich left early, and delivered his verdict to the company.[14] This left Griffith free to roam, and he became only the second European to visit the Mishmi Mountains.[15] Then in 1837 he vanished, and newspapers carried stories of his assassination. Wallich's response to this news is lost to posterity. A year later, however, a battered and dishevelled Griffith staggered across the border out of Burma, having survived a dangerous and illegal collecting trip taking in the Hokong Valley, Ava and Rangoon. His discoveries included *R. griffithianum*, which would eventually exceed *R. arboreum* in its contribution to horticulture, and *R. grande*. He would later botanize and collect in the Khasi Hills, Bhutan, Afghanistan, Simla and Hindoo Koosh, before finally falling in love with Malacca, where he chose to settle.[16]

In 1842 poor health forced Wallich to take a two-year break from Calcutta, and Griffith was summoned back from his beloved Malacca to act as caretaker manager in his absence. Griffith promptly wrote a report on Wallich's 'mismanagement' of the garden and set about radically redesigning it along what he felt were more scientific lines. When Wallich returned in 1844, the garden was his pet no longer. Large numbers of trees had been felled, and others badly damaged.

The latter included the very rare *Amherstia nobilis*, precious to Wallich because he himself had discovered it on one of his few trips into the wild. A demoralized Wallich stayed on for three more years, then left for the last time, retiring to his adopted home of London.[17]

Griffith returned to Malacca in 1844 to begin a settled married life, but had little time to enjoy it, for he died of liver disease less than a year later. A meticulous and energetic worker, Griffith had used every evening of his travels to examine, dissect, describe and illustrate the plants he had found. According to McClelland, his companion in Assam,

> even on his death bed his microscope stood beside him, with the unfinished drawings and papers and dissections on which he was engaged the day on which the fatal symptoms of his disorder came on.[18]

Wallich's insistence that Chinese tea should be grown at Assam would lead indirectly to another extremely useful *Rhododendron* species

'Mrs Duffield' — a cultivar of *Rhododendron griffithianum*.

entering cultivation. By 1838 China was locked into a co-dependent relationship with Britain and the East India Company. The Brits were addicted to tea, and the Company paid for it largely by peddling opium to the Chinese people, smuggling it via a thriving Chinese black market.[19] An understandably miffed Chinese government rebelled but lost, and in consequence was forced in 1842 to open up coastal land to foreign visitors.

The Horticultural Society in 1843 sent a collector called Robert Fortune to China, but with his range limited, he mainly bought plants from local nurseries, including some *Tsutsusi* azaleas. Then, as he sailed south from Shanghai, he faced terrible danger. Ahead lay five pirate ships, against which his own boat had no defence. Fortune lay below decks with a severe fever. The sailors were terrified; it seemed an inescapable situation.[20]

Before setting out, Fortune had won an argument with his sponsors that he should be allowed to carry a shotgun. Now he rose from his bed, seeing a slim chance. Fortune ordered his crew at gunpoint to remain at their posts, for speed was essential. He waited until the first pirate ship was in optimal range, and then fired his shotgun into their massed ranks. He was lucky: the shocked pirates scattered, and Fortune's ship sailed past. Two days later they faced six pirate ships, but Fortune had members of his crew dress in his spare clothes and carry levers as if they were guns. This time when he fired, the pirates thought there were more of these fearsome alien warriors aboard, and took flight.[21]

Fortune wrote a book about his exploits, which caused a sensation back home, catching the attention of the East India Company.[22] Following Wallich's verdict on Assam, they needed a man to acquire, or rather steal, some tea seeds from China. The Chinese, understandably, shielded their precious monopoly, so Fortune disguised himself as a Chinese man and sneaked inland, accompanied by translators who would always claim Fortune was from a distant part of China. Tea growers willingly gave up their seeds and secrets, quite unaware that they were betraying their country. The seeds in the end proved useless, for Griffith had been right and native Assam tea grew better in Assam.[23] However, it was the methodology Fortune learned for making perfect black tea that would break the Chinese monopoly and establish a rival Assam tea industry. Fortune aided this further by bringing to Assam many Chinese expert tea growers; how these men coped with being permanently uprooted to a foreign land is an untold story. From Fortune's tea-hunting trips came another of the most important rhododendrons ever introduced: the sweet-scented *R. fortunei*.

Excluding azaleas, the introduction of rhododendrons into cultivation can be broken down into three significant phases, each more than doubling the available species count. The first was everything up to 1848, and the third was the exploration of China in the early twentieth century. In the middle came 28 species from just one man.

Joseph Dalton Hooker was the son of William, director of Kew. He planned to make a full exploration of the Himalayan kingdom of Sikkim, which neither Wallich nor Griffith had been able to visit. Yet he would face a cunning adversary whom Hooker would describe as 'unsurpassed for insolence and avarice'.[24]

Sikkim had an ageing rajah, but in practical terms the dewan (prime minister) had all the power. Fearing that these British interlopers might interfere with his various dodges and moneymaking schemes, he did everything he could to obstruct Hooker, delaying him for months in Darjeeling. When Hooker finally set off in October 1848, his entourage contained 56 people, of various ethnic origins. They journeyed through tropical forests to Mywa Gola, then ascended over six days to the subalpine village of Wallanchoon, peopled by ethnic Tibetans. Beset by hunger (certain of his men were stealing most of the food), headaches and altitude sickness, Hooker's party continued across the great mountains, gathering rhododendron seeds at as high as 4,000 m (13,100 ft) despite cold fingers and out-of-reach branches.[25]

Hooker's second expedition began on 3 May 1849, but the dewan inserted 'guides' into Hooker's party, with instructions to make their route as tortuously long as possible. Hooker was wise to the plan and tried to win the spies over, and some of these diversions at least led to finding rare plants. The dewan began dismantling infrastructure, taking down bridges and stepping stones, blocking roads and banning repairs.[26] This greatly reduced the amount of food reaching Hooker's party, but for Hooker, that wasn't the worst of it:

> Alas, one of my finest collections of rhododendrons sent to Darjeeling got ruined by coolies falling ill and being detained on the road, so I have to collect the troublesome things afresh. If your shins were as bruised as mine tearing through the interminable rhododendron scrub of 10,000–13,000 feet you would be as sick of the sight of these glories as I am.[27]

A journey that should have taken one month ended up taking three, through leech-infested country. Hooker's flagging spirits were lifted in October when his good friend Dr Archibald Campbell joined their party. Campbell was the British Superintendent of Darjeeling,[28] for whom Hooker named the magnificent *Magnolia campbellii*. When Hooker revealed the scale of the dewan's scheming against him, a furious Campbell dismissed the worst of the dewan's spies from the party, having first 'blackened his face'. Yet the dewan's influence reached even into Tibet, where a party of locals blocked their path and demanded a conference. Campbell obliged, but Hooker suddenly 'put spurs to my pony and galloped ahead to the sandy plains of Tibet'.[29] He botanized there for a day before anyone found him, then three more with Campbell and a Tibetan officer whose friendship had been bought with rum.[30]

Soon afterwards, in a region awash with rhododendrons, Hooker's evening rest was disturbed by a cry for help from Campbell. The sacked spy, the singtam soubah, had returned to implement a new, most vicious plot. Hooker was held back from trying to help Campbell, but caught sight of him striking out with his fists, and struggling violently; being tall and powerful he had already prostrated a few, but a host of men bore down on him.[31]

Eventually Campbell was tightly and painfully bound. The soubah told Hooker he was free to go, but as the party took their captive towards Tumlong, Hooker stayed 'as near as I was allowed, quietly gathering Rhododendron seeds along the way'.[32] Somewhere in England's gardens may grow great rhododendron plants derived from this very seed, their presence there owing to Hooker's refusal to abandon his friend.

The dewan wrote a letter to the British listing his demands, but it was so long and rambling that the translator didn't read as far as the crucial point about Campbell being held hostage.[33] The letter was left for Campbell to deal with on his return, and therefore weeks passed with no response. Eventually, the soubah allowed Hooker to write a letter himself, directly to the Governor-General Lord Dalhousie (after whose wife *R. dalhousiae* is named).

Kidnapping and hostage-taking might have been an accepted negotiating tactic in Nepalese and Tibetan conflicts, but the proud British promptly sent a military force to Darjeeling with an ultimatum: release Campbell immediately, or face invasion.[34] The captors' party now proceeded towards Darjeeling with all the sluggish reluctance of a schoolboy sent to the headmaster's office for punishment. Hooker (now also a captive) and Campbell probably feared at times that they would be killed, either to silence them or simply in a fit of panic. They were finally released on Christmas Eve.[35] The dewan's power was broken, and the British went on to annex southern Sikkim in revenge.[36]

Hooker distributed seed from his discoveries and publicized them with two lavishly illustrated books.[37] He was ably assisted by the young botanist Thomas Thomson, for whom he would name *R. thomsonii*, one of five Hooker finds that adorn his memorial tablet in St Anne's Church on Kew Green. Hooker went on to succeed his father

Rhododendron thomsonii, which Joseph Hooker named after his able assistant Thomas Thomson. An image of this plant adorns a memorial plaque to Hooker in St Anne's Church on Kew Green.

A painting of
*Rhododendron
campylocarpum* by the
great botanist Joseph
Hooker, who also
described this species.
This particular form
is called 'Honeybell'.

as director of Kew, and unlike many rhododendron collectors lived
to a ripe old age.[38]

Hooker's 28 new species caused major excitement among British
rhododendrophiles. The species were mostly tender, so they could
only be grown and enjoyed by those fortunate enough to live in a
mild part of Britain. Gardeners from more frost-prone climes had
to wait once more for the hybridizing nurserymen to cross Hooker's
species with frost-tolerant ones. F_1 hybrids could be generated in
large numbers, if the buyer could accept a degree of uncertainty about
the outcome. Hence earlier plants sold as 'Nobleanum' were simply
F_1s between *caucasicum* and *arboreum*.[39] However, production of the
best hybrid cultivars, the particular selected clones, took far longer.

The pace of life was slower in those days, which was just as well
for these nurserymen. It could take a decade for seeds to produce a
shrub ready to flower naturally, but the wait could be reduced dramatically by grafting a sapling onto a mature plant of another species. In
this way, Standish and Noble at Sunningdale Nurseries saw the first
flowers of *R. thomsonii* in 1857, and immediately began raising hybrids

from it, creating 'Ascot Brilliant' barely a decade after Hooker introduced *thomsonii*.[40]

However, to judge the worth of any given hybrid, a plant grown naturally to flowering age was needed. Moreover, because hybrid cultivars can only be replicated by cuttings or grafting, only twelve new plants per year could be produced at first, which would each themselves take five years before they flowered and could be sold. Hence it might have taken another fifteen years before 'Ascot Brilliant' was available to buy, and then with so few plants available, nurserymen could charge a very high price for near exclusivity. It would typically take another twenty years for the price to drop to something more affordable; in 1886 the newest cultivars cost ten shillings and sixpence, whereas older ones, even the celebrated like 'Lady Eleanor Cathcart', were less than a quarter of the price.[41] Hence over the twenty years following Hooker's travels, over £700 million was reportedly spent on rhododendrons, equalling Britain's national debt.[42] In 1885 James Veitch & Sons (by no means rhododendron specialists) listed for sale more than 200 rhododendron cultivars, plus separate lists of azaleas and vireyas.

Rhododendrons travelled around Europe, and to and from North America. In 1896 an entire stock of 200 seedlings of R. *griffithianum* hybrids were offered for sale in Berlin, and bought by the Dutch Van Nes Nursery.[43] Among these was 'Queen Wilhelmina', a beautiful scarlet-coloured cultivar that would be parent or ancestor to many more, including the very popular 'Britannia'.[44]

One rhododendron cultivar produced by the Waterer dynasty stands above all others, at least in terms of commercial success. Aged seventy, John Waterer had a particular individual cross between 'George Hardy' and 'Broughtonii' that he believed would eclipse anything he'd produced before. As it prepared to flower, his son Gomer made daily pilgrimages to see how this most precious specimen had progressed. Then one day, it was gone!

Nurserymen of the day were careful and secretive, for their new hybrids were both trade secrets and potential fortunes. This is probably why the parentage of many early hybrids is unrecorded. Hence this vanishing act had to be an inside job, or a fluke. Nursery employees did sometimes take home the odd hybrid as a perk of the job, and not all knew which plants were precious. Sure enough, after several days of cold sweat and searching, the plant turned up in the front garden of an employee's cottage, and was duly returned.[45]

Though John would not live to see it, the plant was worth the trouble. Its pink flowers faded with age, but in a stroke of branding genius, Gomer chose the name 'Pink Pearl', turning this into a virtue. Easy to remember and prettier than, say, 'Broughtonii' or 'Blandyanum', this name undoubtedly helped its success with the public.[46] It won awards and the public praise of Queen Alexandra.[47] Then racehorse owner Fred Hardy ordered a whopping 150 of them from Gomer, confident of selling some to his friends, after which Gomer never had to advertise the plant again.[48] It was still a best-seller in 1937. Even in 1963 it was described as 'the only name people know' for a hybrid rhododendron, regardless of its having been superseded in

'Queen Wilhelmina', a bright red hybrid of R. *griffithianum*, whose birth in Berlin is shrouded in mystery.

The 'Pink Pearl', the most commercially successful rhododendron hybrid of all time.

quality.[49] Unlike fragile, high-maintenance beauties such as the 'Loderi' group, 'Pink Pearl' was utterly dependable, and anyone could grow it. It is still on sale today.

Inevitably, mass popularity brought scorn and contempt. By 1954 some regarded it as 'the lowest of the low',[50] the cultivar equivalent of *R. ponticum*. To a later commentator, it formed with 'Nobleanum Venustum' and 'Cynthia' a hideous triumvirate of 'bloated heads of rubbery blooms of knickers-pink, dildo-cream and gingivitis-red'.[51] No plant can hope to please everyone.

Ironically, a few of the detractors of 'Pink Pearl' may well have been happily growing some of its progeny. Plants like 'Souvenir de Doctor S. Endtz' and 'J. G. Millais' had names to appeal to the connoisseur, just as 'Pink Pearl' did to the everyman. 'Pink Pearl' crossed the water to Holland and North America to sire many of its children,[52] and a genealogy of recent American cultivar 'White Ginger' shows the importance of 'Pink Pearl', and also *R. catawbiense*, which is ancestor to all but two of the family tree.

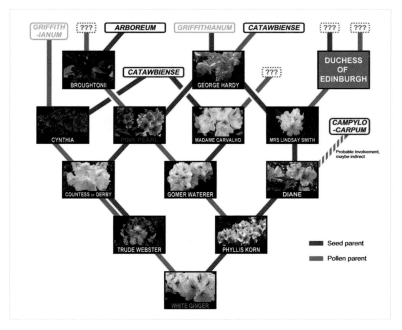

An illustrative genealogy of rhododendron hybrids involving 'Pink Pearl'.
Note how only three or four species are certainly involved, whereas in
four places a parent's identity is unknown.

The bonanza of rhododendron hybrids raised and sold during Victorian times was based upon a small cluster of species. Excluding azaleas and vireyas (which had their own quite separate histories in gardens; see chapters Two and Four), about fifty *Rhododendron* species had been introduced by 1960. Among these, just nine species have dominated the production of rhododendron hybrids, accounting for about 85 per cent of recorded instances of direct or indirect ancestry between them.[53] Each had something specific to offer; of the pre-Hooker species, *catawbiense*, *maximum* and *caucasicum* gave hardiness, *ponticum* vigour, and *arboreum* tall stature plus reddish flowers. Only three of the nine came from Hooker: *griffithianum* gave the largest flowers, *campylocarpum* offered for the first time a yellow tint, and *thomsonii* had glorious red waxy bell-shaped flowers.[54] Completing the top tier was *fortunei* from China, an all-rounder whose particular virtues were seven petals and scent.

Among the nine, *catawbiense*, *griffithianum* and *fortunei* come out as the most important. The latter two gave the spectacular but half-hardy 'Loderi' siblings (see Chapter One). Breeding in R. *catawbiense* could ensure full hardiness, even when crossed with a tender species, making it the most important shrub ever introduced to Britain, according to Kew curator and woody plant expert W. J. Bean.[55] Examples include 'Cynthia' and 'George Hardy', both hybrids with *griffithianum*. A *thomsonii* x *fortunei* cross gave the almost fully hardy 'Luscombei'. A significant early *catawbiense* x *ponticum* cross was 'Cunningham's White', at first grown for its own sake but now the most popular grafting stock for new cultivars.[56] Before 1910 R. *campylocarpum* was barely used, but from 1924 onwards Walter Slocock of Goldsworth Nurseries

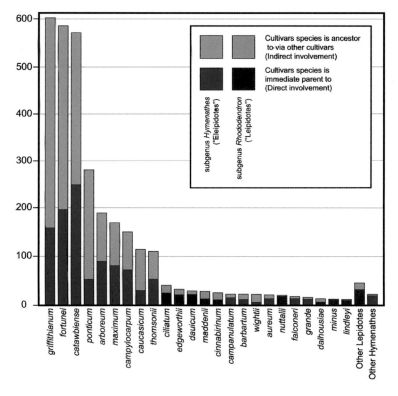

Bar chart showing the number of named cultivars directly and indirectly descended from different *Rhododendron* species, from subgenera *Hymenanthes* (blue) and *Rhododendron* (red), based on data at www.hirsutum.info, accessed August 2015.

'Goldsworth Yellow', an F_1 hybrid between *R. caucasicum* and *R. campylocarpum.*

registered twelve hybrid cultivars from it.[57] He is said to have been a fabulous but brusque character, who marched around his nursery with numerous paper notes pinned to his coat to remind him of what needed doing.[58]

All nine of the top species belong to subgenus *Hymenanthes* ('elepi-dotes'), so Rhododendromania was, more or less, about this group alone. Why, then, was that other great group, the 'lepidotes' of sub-genus *Rhododendron*, nearly ignored? By 1860 about 21 *Hymenanthes* had been introduced, versus thirty lepidotes, hence species availability was not the issue.[59] Some lepidotes were simply lacking in horticul-tural merit, like the alpenroses *ferrugineum* and *hirsutum*, whereas *minus* just looks like a small *R. ponticum*. Generally, lepidotes have smaller flowers than *Hymenanthes*.

The second key point was hardiness, especially for those lepidotes that were otherwise most appealing. All of *dalhousiae, edgeworthii, ciliatum, formosum, maddenii, nuttallii* and *veitchianum* were listed by James Veitch

& Sons in the 1880s as 'stove' or glasshouse plants, alongside the vireyas. The last five belong to the Maddenia group, which combine delicate beauty with some of the best scents in the genus, but most can only be grown outdoors in the mild western extremities of Britain, if at all.[60]

Of course, beauty and hardiness can be combined through hybridization, but Victorian hybridization was very much by trial and error; certainly no one yet knew the simple rule that lepidotes cannot cross with *Hymenanthes*.[61] Breeding programmes were largely based, as we have seen, around a few key species, and the natural course of action for Maddenia species would have been to try and breed them with *R. catawbiense* or its hybrids for hardiness, which would not have worked. Indeed, the more *Hymenanthes* hybrids were produced, the more it would seem that trying to cross Maddenia species with anything but themselves was a lost cause.

This, then, likely accounts for the great overshadowing of lepidotes during Victorian times. For glasshouses, Maddenia species were suitable, but they lacked the crucial advantage of small size enjoyed by the vireyas, nor could such a range of visibly distinct hybrids be raised from among them. They did, however, have one trump card, for they are the smelliest of the 'smellies', or scented rhododendrons.[62] Among the first hybrids involving Maddenia was 'Fragrantissimum' (*edgeworthii* x *formosum*), possibly the most strongly scented rhododendron in existence. One catalogue described it as: 'A most desirable addition; flowers white, tipped with delicate rose; one flower is sufficient to fill with delicious fragrance a good sized house.'[63]

'Fragrantissimum' probably cornered the market on tender scented rhododendrons, despite being 'leggy' (tall and straggly). Most other Maddenia hybrids would come much later, raised where they could survive outdoors such as at Caerhays in Cornwall, or in New Zealand.[64] Had Victorian breeders known the rules, perhaps more would have crossed Maddenia species with the fairly hardy *R. dauricum*. As it is, the only recorded hybrid of this parentage raised before 1927 was 'Praecox', *ciliatum* x *dauricum*, which by hybrid vigour is hardier than either parent.[65] *R. ciliatum* was also successfully crossed with *glaucophyllum* and *virgatum*.[66]

Even among the lepidotes, species seem to cross less readily than within *Hymenanthes*, suggesting greater genetic separation between subgroups of lepidotes. 'Fragrantissimum improved' was a repeat of the *edgeworthii* x *formosum* cross, but unlike the original it turned out to be sterile.[67]

Arguably the best individual species among early lepidote introductions is *R. cinnabarinum*, which is half-hardy and unusually can have orange flowers, which delighted the great explorer Kingdon-Ward.[68] Its subspecies and variants may range from yellow to crimson, and between them are involved in at least fifty cultivars, many of them also involving *R. maddenii*, and most raised after 1915.[69] Had *cinnabarinum* been a *Hymenanthes*, it might have been used far more extensively. However, its particular charm, hardiness and range of possible colours perhaps make it a species not easily improved upon by hybridization.

Cultivar creation is a form of art, an attempt to achieve perfection in four dimensions, for their beauty shifts over time. Some

Rhododendron 'Fragrantissimum' at Trebah, Cornwall. Possibly the strongest scented rhododendron cultivar in existence. The name would not be allowed under current cultivar naming conventions, because it sounds too much like a species.

Colour forms
of *Rhododendron
cinnabarinum*.
The leftmost three,
including the darkest
one, are subspecies
cinnabarinum; the other
four are ssp. *xanthocodon*.
Both may be orange
or magenta, and
colour is not useful
for telling the
subspecies apart.

rhododendron cultivars also bear magnificent names; for example,
'Hello Dolly', 'Holy Moses', 'Jingle Bells', 'Miniskirt', 'Oz', 'Potato
Peeler', 'Smiley's Pinkadilly', 'Walloper', 'Whopper', 'Witchdoctor' and
'Wizard' are all the creations of the irrepressible American hybridizer Halfdan Lem.[70] 'Potato Peeler' was inspired by a customer who
proclaimed that he would need to peel large numbers of potatoes to
cover the bill for his plants.

The French seemed to prefer painting rhododendrons to breeding them, for the plants turn up in a 1922 painting of the Palace of
Versailles (the American artist William Posey Silva's *Rhododendron-
Versailles*), and in Edouard Manet's *Spring* (1881). Manet's health was
failing by this time, yet the painting bursts with young life as its title
suggests. The rhododendrons are very much the backdrop; one (top
left) is in flower but it is barely noticeable, and removing it would

Left: the common mallow, *Malva sylvestris*, whose French name *mauve* gives its name to this colour. Middle: garments dyed with mauveine. Right: *Rhododendron niveum*, which fell from favour when the colour mauve became too common.

not change the feel of the painting. Its main subject, young actress Jeanne Demarsy, looks as if she would not welcome the competition for attention. She radiates a quiet determination to succeed, and would later enjoy fleeting glory in Offenbach's *Orphée aux enfers*, playing Venus; however, the painting would far eclipse her. It was the last great Manet painting to leave private hands, sold for a record $65 million to the Jean Paul Getty Museum.[71]

Just as rhododendrons influenced painters, so events outside of horticulture affected the popularity of certain rhododendrons. Aged just eighteen, William Perkin had been trying to synthesize the expensive antimalarial drug quinine from aniline, a far cheaper chemical that was an easily available extract from coal tar. He failed, but instead created a strong purple dye. Showing remarkable entrepreneurial spirit, he brought it to market as the first ever synthetic dye, mauveine.[72] It surged in popularity after Queen Victoria wore it in 1858, and mauveine even affected the English language, bringing the French word 'mauve' into common use ('mauve' is the French word for the common mallow, *Malva sylvestris*). Mass production made mauveine progressively cheaper, and *Punch Magazine* was soon complaining of women afflicted by 'Mauve Measles'.[73]

Soon even the working classes could afford to wear dye-coloured clothes for the very first time, as long as they were purple, which inevitably made the upper classes turn against the colour. At the same time,

Edouard Manet, *Spring*, 1881, oil on canvas, featuring young actress Jeanne Demarsy in front of Rhododendrons, with a flower visible in the top left corner.

R. ponticum was becoming increasingly ubiquitous (see Chapter Eight), all of which meant that purple rhododendrons were suddenly seen as vulgar. A major casualty of this was *R. niveum*, a purple-flowered species introduced by Hooker.[74] This previously popular species fell dramatically from favour, and was purged from many gardens, although spectacular specimens remain in the Lost Gardens of Heligan.

four
Glasshouse Sensations
❦

The sterling qualities of this splendid group of Hybrid Rhododendrons as decorative plants for the warm greenhouse and
conservatory are now so generally accepted that the following
brilliant additions will, we are persuaded, be received with no
less approval than their predecessors.

JAMES VEITCH & SONS' CATALOGUE, 1892

W e tend to think of rhododendrons as outdoor plants,
but in fact more than one-quarter of all known species
are tropical, and in temperate climates can be grown
only in glasshouses. Almost all of these belong to the vireya group,
which nowadays are grown only by dedicated enthusiasts, though they
were very popular in Victorian times. Remarkably, this popularity
was almost entirely down to the efforts of just one extraordinary
family of plantsmen.

The story began in 1768, when a sixteen-year-old John Veitch
sailed from Scotland to London to take up an apprenticeship with
James Lee, a fellow Scot and one of the leading nurserymen of the
day. Lee was a talented gardener and businessman, and saw similar
potential in Veitch. Two years after hiring Veitch, Lee sent him to
Killerton, near Exeter, to create a landscape garden for the new owner,
Sir Thomas Acland Dyke.[1]

Nine years later, Veitch had not only made great strides with the
garden, but was selling off excess seedlings to neighbours, at a profit

Rhododendron hyacinthosmum, native to New Guinea, is one of the vireya rhododendrons.

for the estate. Sir Thomas then made him head steward, offering a secure job for life and the use of some land for the rest of his life. He further suggested that Veitch might set up his own nursery business.[2] Possibly Sir Thomas, who had recently lost his own adult son, was transferring some of his paternal instincts towards his reliable gardener.

By 1808 Veitch's fledgling business was going well. His two surviving sons, Thomas and James, both had a knack for plants, and worked for the nursery (his eldest had died at Trafalgar). Moreover, James also shared, or even eclipsed, his father's flair for business. While John had grown into a plump, affable and witty man, James was slim, quick-thinking, shrewd and perhaps a little neurotic.[3] Crucially, he also had a passionate interest in exotic plants, which would shape the nursery's future.

By 1826 their nursery had numerous employees, and began winning awards for its plants. The nursery business at the time was ruthless and cutthroat, and the best plantsmen were valued like today's top footballers. Hence Veitch scored a major coup by successfully poaching the talented nurseryman John Dominy away from a rival business.[4] James constantly sought new plants, but avenues for introduction at the time were limited, for plant transport was expensive and ineffective, and Kew was going through a torpid period.[5]

The invention of the Wardian Case or terrarium in 1830 massively improved the chances of getting plants home alive. These were portable, self-contained, hermetically sealed glass cases in which the water transpired by the plants would condense on the glass walls, then run down to the soil for them to drink again. Provided the cases were positioned on the boat with care, plants could survive year-long sea voyages, and could grow from seeds into small plants, saving time for nurserymen.[6] By 1841 Kew was beginning to revive thanks to William Hooker and John Lindley, and James had joined the Horticultural Society, establishing a regular correspondence with Hooker at Kew.[7] James was now ready to send commercial collectors out to get new plants.

Veitch had a young and extremely capable nurseryman called Thomas Lobb, who had worked for Veitch since his mid-teens.[8] Perhaps Veitch considered sending Thomas, but he seems to have been fond of his young charge, and the recent deaths of two gardeners sent by the Duke of Devonshire to Canada may have swayed him against it.[9] Instead, Veitch sent Thomas's older, more rugged brother William to the Americas in 1840. Like Thomas, he had been a plant enthusiast since childhood, and was now a skilled gardener with an urge to travel.[10] William collected all across the Americas; he was the first to bring the giant redwood (*Sequoiadendron giganteum*) to Europe, and the monkey puzzle (*Araucaria araucana*) into commercial use.[11] Another of his introductions, *Rhododendron occidentale*, was critical in the development of the Knap Hill, Exbury and subsequent azalea groups (see Chapter Two). William also brought *Rhododendron* 'Cornish Early Red' (*ponticum* x *arboreum*) to the palace of the Brazilian emperor.[12]

William's success inspired Veitch to create a second expedition, targeting the Old World. This time he did send Thomas, though he

Rhododendron occidentale, introduced by William Lobb, a species unremarkable on its own but which was critical to the development of Knap Hill, Exbury and subsequent azalea groups.

Rhododendron malayanum, the first vireya species to be discovered and described.

was anxious that the delicate young man should not have to mix with common sailors (he had had no such concerns about William). After a very long sea voyage, Thomas arrived in Singapore in June 1843. His goal was Java, but he was blocked for a year by local bureaucracy, something modern botanical collectors are all too familiar with, so he began his explorations in the Malay Peninsula.[13]

At the time, the only vireya rhododendron known to science was *R. malayanum*.[14] By 1861 Thomas Lobb had discovered four more species, *javanicum*, *jasminiflorum*, *brookeanum* and *longiflorum* (= *lobbii*), and sent living material of all five to Veitch. In fact, both Veitch and Lobb were more interested in orchids, but these had a frustrating tendency to die in transit, whereas the rhododendrons survived to give Veitch some return on his investment.[15]

Thanks to Joseph Hooker, rhododendrons were about to become big business, but when Lobb came to India he judged them too risky and expensive to go after – a costly mistake.[16] Lobb made up for it, however, by supplying for Veitch the magnificent orchid *Vanda coerulea*, and the lily *Cardiocrinum giganteum*,[17] whose enormous size makes it perfect for growing among large rhododendron plantings.

The Crystal Palace exhibition of 1851 helped stimulate a boom in glasshouse plants among Victorians. While many nurseries could compete to supply orchids and begonias, only Veitch had vireyas. Veitch set to work skilled hybridizers like John Dominy and John Heal. Two further species, *R. teysmannii* and *R. multiflorum*, were introduced from Borneo in 1880, making seven in total.[18] From these, more than 150 distinct hybrids had been bred by 1891.

As well as adorning many a Victorian glasshouse, the hybrid vireyas raised by the Veitch Nurseries helped to advance scientific understanding at the time. In 1891 the Reverend Professor G. Henslow, a major botanical thinker of the time, stood up to deliver a lecture to the Royal Horticultural Society.[19] In it, he would amply summarize what was known about the rules of character inheritance among plants at the time, dispelling some myths, and adding new insights.

Cardiocrinum giganteum, a lily collected by Thomas Lobb and offered for sale by the Veitches. Its huge size and similar ecology makes it perfect for planting among rhododendrons, and it flowers after most rhododendrons have finished, in June. Fine displays can be seen at Edinburgh (pictured) and St Andrews botanic gardens.

His evidence came entirely from vireya hybrids raised by the Veitches. Henslow neatly described why vireyas, and indeed most *Rhododendron* flowers, can be certain colours but not others. Pigments in them were:

> all reducible to two, yellow and rose-red. The former is produced by the presence of yellow granules scattered within the cells of the epidermis or underlying tissue; while the reds are due to the various degrees of concentration of a coloured fluid both in individual cells and by superposition of cells containing the rose-coloured fluid.[20]

Thus the two primary colours of rhododendron flowers are produced by quite different cellular mechanisms. Oranges and bright reds are made by combining both kinds, and colour variation across a flower's petals results from varying intensity of one or both pigment types. Therefore, crossing a pink with a yellow often gives red or orange progeny; however, sometimes a gene from one species can turn off or on a pigment gene from another, creating an unexpected outcome. Hence when white-flowered *R. jasminiflorum* and orange *R. javanicum* were crossed, the offspring ('Princess Royal' and 'Jasminiflorum Carminatum') were pink.[21]

If an F_1 hybrid is backcrossed to one parent species, then only half of the genes from the other species will be retained, but exactly which genes remain will differ between offspring, leading to great variation between individuals. Hence backcrosses from 'Princess Royal' to *R. javanicum* could be rose pink, creamy white or yellow-white.[22] However, Veitch's team often crossed their F_1 hybrids with a third species, and then a fourth in subsequent generations.

The reasoning behind this particular method of hybridization, Henslow explained, was that always having one pure species as parent to any individual guaranteed good quality, especially for colour.[23] This, we now know, ensured that the hybrid would have one complete set of genes from that particular species, ensuring vigour and health, plus a random assemblage of genes from several others, conferring a unique set of characters. Crossing any two hybrids, conversely, risks 'hybrid breakdown', a loss of fitness due to an absence of key genes, and the Veitch hybridizers rarely did it.[24]

Henslow also observed from these crosses how some colour shades could reappear after skipping a generation. 'Taylorii' shared a pink colour with its grandparent 'Princess Royal', but its immediate parents were the pinkish-white 'Princess Alexandra' and the straw-coloured *R. brookeanum* var. *gracile*.[25]

A common misconception about hybridization is that it creates mutations; that is, changes to the DNA that can alter or disable gene function. This is untrue; mutations happen at a slow rate in every generation of every organism on Earth, although the rate can be accelerated by factors like radiation. When unexpected characters show up in hybrids, it is usually due to the mixing of genes, and/or the effect of one gene upon another.

On rare occasions, however, mutations can occur by chance in a hybrid plant, as in any other individual. One of the best of Veitch's team, John Heal, noticed a single mutant stamen on a single flower of a second generation hybrid, whose exact identity is unrecorded but probably involved *javanicum*, *jasminiflorum* and *brookeanum*. Heal deliberately self-pollinated this exact flower, and was rewarded with an extraordinary array of offspring, which collectively were termed the 'Balsamaeflorum' section. Some of these had flowers that were fully double, while others were single, and one had flowers of each kind on different parts of the plant. Colours ranged from white to crimson via various shades of pink, and red to yellow via shades of orange; flower and leaf shape were also highly variable. Henslow observed that if a double-flowered individual was crossed with a single one, the offspring was always single;[26] he was describing the same dominant-recessive pattern of gene expression discovered by the geneticist monk Mendel in his famous peas (Mendel's work at the time still languished undiscovered in an obscure journal).

The second half of the nineteenth century was a high point for both Veitches and vireyas. The Veitch family acquired new premises in Chelsea in 1853, and were then able to display their plants to potential customers from London.[27] James Veitch had five sons, but three of them went abroad and another, William, had to be forced to participate in the business, with predictably unsatisfactory results.[28] Only James Junior shared his father's skills and acumen, and was given the Chelsea branch to run while James Senior stayed in Exeter. Ten years later James Senior died, and his prodigal son Robert took over the Exeter branch, which became principally a tree nursery.[29] The businesses separated, leaving James Junior to lead the way in hybridizing vireyas with his team in Chelsea.

However, James Junior seemed to lack his father's easy rapport with collectors. William Lobb had eventually settled in California, where he died alone, while Thomas had lost contact with the Veitch family around the time James Senior died, in 1863. However, six years later Thomas came to London to meet James Junior. What they talked about is a matter of conjecture, but James might have wanted Thomas to return to collecting, while Thomas might have been angry

Four cultivars from the Balsamaeflorum group, all from the same self-pollinated flower. Top left: 'Rajah'; top right, 'Album'; bottom left, 'Carneum'; bottom right, 'Aureum'.

at the treatment of his brother, or even a lack of support for himself, after an injury sustained while collecting left him unable to work. They had a furious row, and James died from a heart attack later that night.[30] Understandably, James's children had no further contact with Thomas, but his grandson James Herbert Veitch gave both brothers due credit in *Hortus Veitchii*, a definitive record of the family company's plants, people and activities.[31]

James Junior left three sons, among them John Gould Veitch, one of only two Veitches to do his own collecting. He introduced more than 500 plants from the Philippines and Polynesia, but at great cost, for he died from tuberculosis aged just 31.[32] His youngest brother, Arthur, also died fairly young, in 1880; Robert's son Peter had also worked for the Chelsea firm until 1878, when he left to help his ageing father at the Exeter nursery. This left James Junior's middle son, Harry, as the only adult male in a large family, with a business to run.[33] John's son James Herbert Veitch would later also go collecting, bravely undaunted by his father's fate; his introductions included *R. schlippenbachii*.[34]

As the century turned and the Edwardian age began, vireyas were falling from favour. They could not leave the glasshouse, nor compete with the multiplying orchids within them. The Veitches themselves hastened the vireyas' decline by sending Ernest 'Chinese' Wilson to China, bringing back the first wave of rhododendrons that were both fully hardy and truly exotic (see Chapter Five). Most of the vireya cultivars described by Henslow disappeared from cultivation including, sadly, all of the Balsamaeflorums.[35] Furthermore, as each was a unique clone, they can never be recreated, only replaced. Some of those few that survive can be seen in the montane tropics glasshouse in the Royal Botanic Garden, Edinburgh.

At that time the Veitch family also seemed to fall into decline. Neither James Herbert Veitch nor his brother John (a footballer who once scored a hat-trick for England) were suited to running the business, and both were dead by late 1914.[36] This left Harry once again in sole charge, but he was now over sixty and could not go on forever;

he had no children of his own. New tax regimes were squeezing the big estates; meanwhile, plunging transport costs paradoxically hurt the Veitch business, by making imports much more competitive. It was no time for an old man to be running a nursery business. Not wishing to risk a new owner sullying the business name, he chose to close it altogether. There followed one last bonanza for plant-lovers, a closing-down sale including more than 6,000 named rhododendron plants.[37]

The Exeter business kept going, now run by Robert's son Peter, but war soon took its toll. Large numbers of gardeners were joining up, their names listed in regular 'Roll of Honour' pages in the *Gardeners' Magazine* from 1914 onwards. For example, the edition of 31 October 1914 listed 116 'Horticulturists' who had gone to serve. Among those listed was Peter's son J. Leonard Veitch. He survived the Somme and several other battles, won a Military Cross and rose to the rank of major, but was eventually killed in action in 1918, while

Rhododendron 'Triumphans,' one of the few survivors from the vireya cultivars raised by Veitch nurseries.

The front page of the auction catalogue signifying the end for James Veitch and Sons, Ltd as a business.

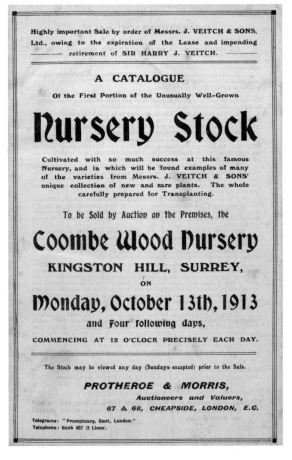

Highly important Sale by order of Messrs. J. VEITCH & SONS, Ltd., owing to the expiration of the Lease and impending ——— retirement of SIR HARRY J. VEITCH. ———

A CATALOGUE

Of the First Portion of the Unusually Well-Grown

Nursery Stock

Cultivated with so much success at this famous Nursery, and in which will be found examples of many of the varieties from Messrs. J. VEITCH & SONS' unique collection of new and rare plants. The whole carefully prepared for Transplanting.

To be Sold by Auction on the Premises, the

Coombe Wood Nursery

KINGSTON HILL, SURREY,

ON

Monday, October 13th, 1913

and Four following days,

COMMENCING AT 12 O'CLOCK PRECISELY EACH DAY.

The Stock may be viewed any day (Sundays excepted) prior to the Sale.

PROTHEROE & MORRIS,

Auctioneers and Valuers,

67 & 68, CHEAPSIDE, LONDON, E.C.

Telegrams: "Promptuary, Cent, London."
Telephone: Bank 857 (2 Lines).

in temporary charge of the 1st Battalion Devonshire Regiment.[38] His death left his sister Anna Mildred to succeed Peter, becoming the last Veitch Nursery owner. She kept the Exeter business going until 1969, when failing health forced her to sell it to St Bridget Nurseries.[39]

The Veitches are now recalled only in horticultural history books, albeit occupying a most prominent role. The vireyas, on the other hand, have enjoyed a modest renaissance. Dozens more species have been imported, and hundreds described. Moreover, one no longer has to be a rich man to own a warm glasshouse. Needless to say, with so much more raw material available, the number of hybrids is now legion.[40]

Lurking as they do mainly in the high branches of tropical rainforest trees, vireyas evade discovery far more effectively than other *Rhododendron* species. Consequently, while the discovery of a genuinely new *Rhododendron* species from any other group is a rare event, new vireyas are still popping up from time to time. Already 313 species have been described, most of them not yet in cultivation.[41] Scientists have also begun to unpick the history of this remarkable group, building an evolutionary tree by sampling DNA from as many species as possible.[42]

From this we know that vireyas are a specialized offshoot of the lepidote rhododendrons (subgenus *Rhododendron*). The first vireya species to diverge was the anomalous *R. santapaui*, known from just two localities in India's Arunachal Pradesh.[43] From here they marched southward from the east Himalayan foothills towards the islands of tropical Asia, leaving behind a cluster of species called the pseudo-vireyas. These have some of the smallest flowers of any rhododendrons, and include *R. kawakamii*, *R. quadrasianum* and *R. retusum*.

Having reached the islands of tropical Asia, vireyas began an explosive process of diversification, with various evolutionary lines repeatedly dispersing between islands, and sometimes back again. Separation by sea encouraged different populations to follow distinct evolutionary paths, adapting to specific habitats and pollinators, leading, for example, to rapid changes in flower colour and shape. Indeed, species that look similar have often turned out not to be closely related, for convergent evolution can give two unrelated plants similar flowers if both are using the same pollinator. The process of island-hopping evolution is still very much ongoing, for species like *R. javanicum*, *R. jasminiflorum*, *R. malayanum* and *R. zollingeri* are spread across many of the islands, and the different geographical colour forms of *R. javanicum* may be on their way to becoming separate species themselves.

New Guinea has a subtly different story. Vireyas are exceptionally diverse there, with 88 species in Papua alone.[44] Nearly all of these descend from a single common ancestor that arrived there within the last 15 million years.[45] There has been very little immigration of

Vireya group rhododendrons from New Guinea. Left to right and top to bottom: *anagalliflorum, baenitzianum, bagobonum, blackii, christi, christianae, commonae, curviflorum, gracilentum, hyancinthosmum, konori var. phæopeplum, leptanthum, loranthiflorum, macgregoriae, pleianthum, rarum, solitarium, stevensianum, superbum, vitis-idaea.*

vireyas since, and no detectable emigration of species except into Australia. This is part of a larger pattern first detected among animals by the great naturalist Alfred Russell Wallace: New Guinea and its surrounding islands have very different plant and especially animal communities from those further west. This is because New Guinea is part of the Australian tectonic plate, and only recently moved into close proximity to Borneo and the more westerly islands. Moreover, New Guinea has a very complex geological history; most of what now exists might have been underwater 20 million years ago.[46] If so, New Guinea might have acquired its first vireya long after the group had diversified across all of the islands to the west. This new arrival would have encountered a young and developing rainforest ecosystem and diversified rapidly to fill all available ecological niches, demonstrating the explosive power of evolution within *Rhododendron*.

In strict evolutionary terms, vireyas are merely a group within a group within *Rhododendron*.[47] However, they are distinct in appearance and easily recognized. They are not quite the only epiphytes, but other than two rare members of subgenus *Hymenanthes* they are the only rhododendrons in the Malesia Archipelago. Many rhododendrophiles are barely aware of the group, but once you've seen them it is easy to be captivated, as the Veitch family and their hybridizers once were.

five

The Home of the Rhododendrons

ॐ

It may be regarded as possible that the Celestial Empire [China]
contains more species of this genus than all the world besides.

J.T.D. LLEWELLYN, 'Hardy Rhododendrons and Azaleas' (1893)

I n the northeastern corner of Yunnan, in southwest China, three
mighty rivers plunge through the landscape, passing within just
80 km (50 miles) of one another. Yet they never meet; the Nu
Jiang or Salween empties into the Gulf of Martaban south of Myanmar,
whereas the Mekong has its delta 1,290 km (800 miles) away in south
Vietnam. The third river, the Yangtze, abruptly turns north then
south again, before meandering northeastwards towards the East
China Sea near Shanghai, more than 2,820 km (1,750 miles) from the
deltas of the other two. In Yunnan, each river has cut a monstrously
deep valley, and they are hence separated from one another by high
mountain ridges. Populations of plants and animals in the different
valleys are likewise isolated from one another, and so have followed
separate evolutionary paths, helping to promote extraordinary diversity in the region.

When the collector George Forrest walked through northeast
Yunnan in the early twentieth century, he formed a belief that among
its highest peaks lurked the true home of the rhododendrons, from
which all other species originated. There, he believed, hundreds of
different *Rhododendron* species might grow together. Yet this was a
one-man myth, a sort of botanical Shangri-La. Forrest was already

standing in the place that has more wild *Rhododendron* species than anywhere else on Earth.

Forrest was one of a handful of collectors who between them would bring hundreds of new *Rhododendron* species into the gardens of the West, hence dwarfing the collections sent by Hooker. All would face great dangers, and some would narrowly escape death, while others were destined to die in Asia, far from home.

Until the mid-nineteenth century, China was a secretive country, largely uninterested in trade with foreigners. A few Russian missions were permitted, and a physician named Kirilov discovered *R. mucronulatum* as a result, but otherwise China allowed only a couple of trading outposts on its coast, and those stationed there were not allowed to wander far. China was forced to open up some coastal land to foreign visitors after losing the First Opium War, in 1842.[1] This led to the discovery of *Rhododendron championae*, and made possible the daring but nefarious exploits of the tea thief Robert Fortune, leading to the introduction of *R. fortunei*, among others.

Following a second brief war in 1860, a new treaty permitted the presence of certain foreigners in all parts of China, particularly officials and missionaries. This made commercial collection possible inland for the first time, but for forty years it barely happened. Promising young botanists Richard Oldham and Augustus Margary died young, though the former did number *R. oldhamii* among his finds. Crucially, Veitch Nurseries collector Charles Maries turned back at Yichang, and therefore never witnessed the amazing plant diversity of Yunnan and thereabouts.[2] Moreover, his spiky personality caused friction with the Chinese, and he reported to the Veitches that the natives were hostile. All this might have been a factor in discouraging further commercial collecting trips to China during Victorian times.[3] This would all change, thanks to two French missionaries.

Père Armand David trained as a Catholic priest, but was encouraged by his enlightened order to continue pursuing his love of natural sciences, and he became an enthusiastic and popular science teacher at Savona College, Italy. However, his deepest desire was to see eastern Asia, and so in 1862 he travelled to Mongolia. French scientists were aware of his rare ability as a naturalist, and implored that he be allowed and encouraged to collect specimens.[4]

In 1869 David came to Sichuan. Here, his humble likeability and respectful behaviour earned him the trust and friendship of the cautious local people, enabling him to penetrate deeper into their land.[5] By the end of his travels in 1874, he had sent back huge numbers of specimens and discovered numerous plants of horticultural import-ance, many of which bear his name, including *Buddleia davidii*, the handkerchief tree *Davidia involucrata, Rhododendron davidii, R. decorum, R. moupinense* and *R. strigillosum*.[6]

David was followed by Père Jean Marie Delavay, an equally efficient collector and naturalist. Both men wandered the hills alone, system-atically recording all that they found, and in doing so discovered thousands of species new to Western science. The great botanist Adrien Franchet wrote an entire book about the new species that had been found by Delavay, including *R. ciliicalyx, R. fastigiatum,*

Rhododendron davidii, one of the many species named after Father Jean Pierre Armand David.

R. irroratum, *R. racemosum* and *R. yunnanense*.[7] Delavay is commemorated in *R. delavayi* (= *R. arboreum* ssp. *delavayi*), one of the most abundant and culturally significant rhododendrons in western China (see Chapter Seven). As befits a man of God, Delavay continued his collections with selfless devotion even after contracting bubonic plague in 1888, finally succumbing to the disease seven years later in Yunnan.[8]

These were by no means the only missionary botanists. Two others who would discover *Rhododendron* species were Père Paul Farges (*R. fargesii*, *R. discolor* and *R. sutchuenense*) and Père Jean Soulié (*R. souliei* and *R. ramosissimum*, now known as *R. nivale*).[9]

The exotic plants found by David and Delavay could be read about, but not grown by gardeners, because the missionaries made no commercial seed collections. Thus grew a new hunger for collections from China. Amateur collector Augustine Henry deepened this hunger by discovering 500 new species while working for the Chinese Customs Service, including at Mengtze in Yunnan.[10] He discovered *R. augustinii* and *R. auriculatum*, and knew a location for *Davidia involucrata*, the plant that English nurseryman Harry Veitch wanted the most.[11] Now all Veitch needed was a brave and skilled young man to go out there and get it.

In 1899 the Kew director recommended to Veitch a student, Ernest Henry Wilson.[12] Wilson spent six months with Veitch learning

Two of the rhododendrons discovered by Wilson: *R. lutescens* and *R. davidsonianum*.

the nursery trade, before travelling to China via North America. Henry was preparing to leave China, so Wilson had to move quickly, but he was held up for weeks by plague outbreaks and local unrest. Finally the two men met, and Henry presented Wilson with a sketch map to the location of a single *Davidia* tree. A small sheet of paper covering an area over 160 km (100 miles) wide, it was not much to go on.[13]

Amateur botanists can travel alone, but commercial collectors need an entourage, for they collect in quantity. Wilson hired translators, cooks and porters, and bought a boat. Sometimes a display of import-ance might be needed to impress or intimidate local bureaucrats, so he purchased two sedan chairs as well. His party sailed up the river to Badong, then proceeded on foot into the hills beyond. There, helpful locals guided him to the exact spot Henry had marked on his map, where a distraught Wilson encountered the stump of a recently felled handkerchief tree.[14]

Despondently, Wilson retreated to Yichang. He collected what he could for his employer in the local hills, where his finds included *Rhodo-dendron decorum*, *R. fargesii* and the so-called kiwi fruit, *Actinidia chinensis*. Then one day he was struggling through thick woodland when he unexpectedly came face to face with *Davidia involucrata*, in full flower. Elated, he returned to Veitch in triumph in 1902.[15]

On his second collecting trip, Wilson faced terrible perils as his boat approached the Yeh-Tan rapids above Yichang, rendered even more fearsome than usual by recent heavy rains. These ripped apart a succession of three boats in front of Wilson's boat, killing everyone aboard. Yet somehow, with a hundred men pulling its ropes, Wilson's boat made it through.[16] He now embarked on an exhausting journey through Tibet, which brought back *Rhododendron calophytum* and *R. lutescens*, two *Cypripedium* species and numerous alpines, including the prized *Meconopsis integrifolia*.

Wilson managed more than a year at home between 1905 and 1906, and was there for his daughter's birth. During a third trip, between 1907 and 1909, he collected *Rhododendron moupinense* and the beautiful regal lily, *Lilium regale*, but the latter's bulbs all rotted before he got them home. Because of this, he went back in 1910, and saw one of the great sights of the botanical world: tens of thousands of *Lilium regale* in flower, covering a normally drab hillside in the arid Min Valley. Joyously he marked the spots for 6,000 of them, to be collected in the autumn. Then he accepted the rare luxury of a ride in a sedan chair as they left the site.[17]

Landslides are a common hazard in upland China, because of earthquakes, and degradation of the hillside vegetation that helps hold the soil together. The first sign of trouble was Wilson's dog, which cowered and flinched. Then rocks started crashing down from the hillside above. Wilson leapt from his chair, just in time to see it smashed to pieces by a huge boulder. The only shelter was some fixed boulders up ahead, and Wilson, like his men, ran towards them. Then a small rock crashed into his leg. He found himself on the ground, unable to move and in intense pain, watching the last of the rocks hurtle by. Had Wilson lost consciousness, his party might have fled, and left him to die. As it was, he managed to bark orders to stay put, and to build him a splint from his camera's tripod. Before he could use it, however, he had to lie still while a large train of mules walked past him, their careful feet landing right in front of his face, but never on his body.[18]

Wilson's leg soon became infected, and he might have died but for two pieces of fortune. The first was that his party had a second sedan chair, which had survived the landslide intact, and in which they carried their tortured leader to Chengdu. The second was the presence there of a Dr W. H. Davidson, who managed to save both Wilson and his leg.[19] Wilson later thanked him by naming R. *davidsonianum* in the doctor's honour.

Such an injury would have finished the collecting careers of many, but not Wilson's. After a few years working in the Arnold Arboretum in Boston, he embarked on two more sedate collecting missions, targeting mainly oriental nurseries, accompanied by his wife and daughter, leading to the introduction of the Kurume azaleas.[20] For

Photograph by Ernest Wilson of his wife and daughter conducting a Japanese tea ceremony.

young Muriel, who was seven when they set out, the experience probably veered between incredible excitement and extreme, prolonged boredom.[21] After this, Wilson enjoyed eleven years in Boston with his family, quietly revelling in the nickname 'Chinese Wilson', which his exploits had earned him among the locals. He wrote numerous scientific and horticultural papers, including several on *Rhododendron*, among them an account of 'azaleas' that was definitive in its day.[22] He would have given much more, but tragically he and his wife died in a car accident in 1930.[23]

Many commercial plant collectors were highly territorial, reacting to the presence of another on their patch in much the same way as a domestic cat. An exception to this was the gregarious Reginald Farrer, whose childhood among the limestone hills of Yorkshire had given him a taste for alpine plants. For his first collecting trip he teamed up with William Purdom, a collector whose modest exploits had been dwarfed by those of Wilson. Together they scoured the eastern edge of the Tibetan Plateau from 1914 to 1915, but it gave rather meagre returns, and many of his collections were quickly lost to cultivation because of the war. Farrer himself spent the rest of the war working for the ministry of information.[24]

After the war, with Yunnan now firmly claimed by Forrest, Farrer went to upper Burma (Myanmar). He collected with Euan Cox during

1919, then continued alone in 1920. He discovered new *Rhododendron* species, and introduced *sperabile, calostrotum* and *campylocarpum* ssp. *caloxanthum*, but these had little impact because Burmese plants tended to struggle in British gardens.[25]

The terrain in Burma had always been challenging, and the relentlessly damp climate more so. Drying out seeds for transport became exceedingly difficult, and finally in October 1920, aged just forty, Farrer succumbed to dysentery.[26] His legacy far exceeds his brief collecting career, thanks to two books he wrote during the war describing his collecting adventures.[27] These would greatly increase desire for Chinese plants in a world emerging from the horrors of war, and help to fuel demand for those collectors who were fated to live longer. Cox, meanwhile, left a touching description of a man who died too young:

> His stocky figure clad in khaki shorts and shirt, tieless and collarless, a faded topee on his head, old boots, and stockings that gradually slipped down and clung about his ankles as the day wore on. The bustle of the early start, the constant use of field-glasses which always hung around his neck . . . his intense satisfaction when a plant was in the collecting tin and found worthy; his grunt of disapproval when it was worthless.[28]

During 1902 a young Scottish man named George Forrest was caught in a downpour while fishing on Gladhouse Loch, south of Edinburgh. Seeking shelter, he noticed an oddly rectangular stone protrusion from a gravelly slope, which turned out to be a prehistoric coffin, complete with skeleton, poking out of a tumulus.[29] This find brought him to the attention of Edinburgh Botanic Garden director Isaac Bayley Balfour. Forrest was already a seasoned traveller with training in making plant specimens,[30] but the only job Balfour could offer was working with pressed specimens at the herbarium, where Forrest met his future wife, Clementina Traill. A year later, Balfour recommended

Forrest as a collector to the nurseryman Arthur Bulley, who was seeking primulas from China.[31]

Forrest reached Dali, Yunnan in 1904, but too late in the year to collect plants. He used the winter months well, learning Chinese and vaccinating the locals against smallpox, winning their friendship and respect. With a trusted team recruited, he set out on his first proper collecting trip in 1905, but he was heading straight into danger.[32]

Both the English and the Chinese had recently made military incursions into Tibet, and now corrupt Tibetan lamas were exciting the population into a bloody revolt. Chinese officials, British nationals and blameless French missionaries were slaughtered – often by horrendous means – and their buildings burnt.[33] Among these was Père Jean Armand Soulié, the discoverer of *R. souliei*.[34] Forrest, however, knew nothing of these events, and had come to the mission house of Pères Dubernard and Bourdonnec in Tzekou (now Cigu) close to the Tibet–Yunnan border.[35]

When news came that the bloodthirsty lamas were heading their way, Forrest's party fled along with everyone who had lived in the mission, including many women and children. A desperate moonlit march of 100 people followed, but their path passed close to a lamasery in Batang, where a single sound from the desperate party was overheard, alerting their enemies. They still had a chance if they moved quickly, but they were delayed by an obstructive village headman. Worse, they came to a rise from which the missionaries looked back to see their mission burning. Their spirits broken, they sat down to await their fate. Desperate to do something constructive, Forrest climbed to a nearby vantage point to see if he could find an escape route for them all. Instead he saw a party of armed Tibetans running along the path towards the party.[36]

Forrest shouted a warning, and his collecting team fled, but all but one were caught. Father Bourdonnec was felled by poison arrows, and most of the missionary party was slaughtered. Suddenly alone, Forrest fled, crashing through dense vegetation that cut his clothes to ribbons. He hid behind a huge rock, readying his rifle for a last

George Forrest, saddled up and ready for action.

stand if he was found, but the Tibetans passed by. That night Forrest made a long climb through unforgiving rocks and jungle, but found the exit to the valley blocked by Tibetans with watch fires and dogs. He spent nine days trapped in the valley, hiding by day and fruitlessly seeking escape by night. He buried his boots for fear that the prints would give him away, but would later pay for this by spearing his foot. Several times he was almost killed or caught, and two poisoned arrows passed through his hat.[37]

On one occasion, it is said that he was saved from discovery thanks to the appearance of Father Dubernard on the slope above him, miming a warning to move downstream. By some accounts, Père Dubernard had been killed three days earlier.[38] Did he rise from the grave to save Forrest? A more rational explanation is that Dubernard evaded capture for a few days before being caught and killed.[39] Either way, the two martyr priests are now honoured by a cathedral and Catholic community in the upper Mekong Valley.[40]

Through all this time, Forrest ate nothing but a few dried peas and wheat grains he had found on the ground. At last, battered, bruised and nearing death from starvation, he staggered towards the nearest village, expecting to have to fight to the death for his food. Yet the people there proved friendly and the headman, 'one of the best friends I ever had', arranged for Forrest to be smuggled to safety over arduous mountain routes, 'cutting our way through miles of rhododendrons' in a botanist's paradise he had no chance to enjoy.[41]

A lesser man might have fled China, but not Forrest. Instead, he went travelling with a friend, Consul Litton, as soon as he had recovered, in October 1905, but Litton succumbed to malaria soon after, and Forrest never again had such a good friend in China.[42] When Forrest himself became ill with malaria later that year, he refused to return home, and instead co-ordinated plant collection from his sickbed.[43] Though he would recover, this set the mould for his future collecting: many (perhaps most) of his collections were actually made by the team of gifted and hardworking local men he had assembled. Their leader was Zhao Chengzhang, whom Forrest knew as Lao Chao ('Old Chao'), and who in return called Forrest 'Old Fu'. Zhao was taxonomically astute, arguing that *R. giganteum* and *R. protistum* were different species, while Forrest disagreed (pleasingly, these are now regarded as distinct varieties of one species, so both were half right). Zhao's team even collected for Forrest when he was back in Scotland, making Zhao arguably the most prolific rhododendron collector of all.[44]

Back home, Forrest married Clementina, and had to turn down a collecting opportunity because it would have meant missing the birth of his first child. Later trips by Forrest began to be funded by groups of backers, and increasingly, these backers were after rhododendrons. By 1920 he had made four trips to China and was credited with introducing more than 100 *Rhododendron* species.[45] Despite this, Forrest had come to believe that he had only scratched the surface.

Forrest reasoned that rhododendrons must have a place of origin, or 'home', from which all species had come, and which would host

Forrest's collecting team, including Zhao Chengzhang (sixth from left), with flowerpresses.

species and diversity hitherto undreamed of. He thought he knew where to go, north of 29°N and west of 98°W, writing that 'travel north-westwards and the species are ever on the increase; break eastwards or south and there is a marked decrease in numbers immediately'.[46] Forrest's mentor, Balfour, encouraged his search, for – right or wrong – it enriched his collections.

Curiously, the beliefs of Forrest's collecting team may have both helped and hindered this quest. They were Naxi, raised on Dongba mythology, and legends of three huge 'black rhododendron' (*R. decorum*) plants growing on Mount Shílo (see Chapter Six). If they thought this was the place Forrest spoke of, they would not have been keen to go there, for in legend it was also the gateway to the world of the dead. However, embedded in their culture was an intimate association with the lay of the land, making them supremely efficient at locating plants. Their work made Forrest the greatest of all rhododendron collectors, but he never found their fabled 'home'. After Balfour died in 1922, his quest to find it withered.[47]

By the end of his sixth trip, in March 1926, Forrest had spent less than 24 months at home during the preceding nine years.[48] Now, finally, he seemed ready to settle down. His appears to have been a genuinely happy marriage – indeed he named *Rhododendron* species after both his wife and her father (*clementinae* and *traillianum*). He spent four happy years with his wife and three children, but by 1930 China was calling to him again. So he planned one more trip, promising that it would certainly be his last.[49]

The expedition started badly, with Forrest forced to endure the reckless and hedonistic behaviour of one of his sponsors, Major Johnson, who had come along for the ride. Johnson caused repeated delays, then terrible stress as his foolish behaviour brought on a near-fatal illness.[50] At last a relieved Forrest went on without him, amassing huge quantities of seed. But the trip took a heavy toll on a man approaching his sixties, and even as he prepared to go home, Forrest dropped dead from a heart attack. He was buried in Yunnan near to his friend Litton.[51] Denied even the comfort of a grave to visit, perhaps Clementina visited instead the many rhododendrons growing in the Royal Botanic Garden, Edinburgh from the seed her husband brought back. With so many species growing side by side, Forrest had in a sense helped to create the very place he had been seeking, a home for rhododendrons.

We now know that Yunnan cannot be the place of origin for rhododendrons, for the simple but remarkable reason that rhododendrons are perhaps 20 million years older than the Himalaya Mountains. Yunnan, in its current form, did not exist when rhododendrons first evolved.

The rhododendron story began around 90 million years ago, when the common ancestor to all of the family Ericaceae (which includes *Rhododendron*) evolved a new way to interact with fungi.[52] Root associations with fungi have probably existed for as long as there have been plants on land, but Ericaceae can form partnerships with a far wider range of fungi than most other plants.[53] For example,

Rhododendrons discovered and named by Forrest: *traillianum* after his father-in-law, and *clementinae* after his wife.

fourteen distinct fungal species were found on the roots of a single *Rhododendron* species in China.[54] Each fungus would deliver different nutrients to the rhododendron, providing a clear advantage where nutrients were hard to obtain. This helps ericaceous plants to succeed in habitats where the soil is poor or acidic, and is key to the ecological dominance of *Rhododendron* in China and elsewhere.[55] Paradoxically, it might even help Chinese species to grow on bare limestone, which, as Forrest noted, so many do.[56]

Fossils tell us that by 60 million years ago *Rhododendron* had evolved and spread to all of central Europe, China and eastern North America.[57] This was before the geological collision between India and Asia that would create the Himalaya Mountains. DNA evidence shows that the first *Rhododendron* species to split from the others was *R. camtschaticum*, a subarctic carpet-forming species with lots of glandular hairs and flowers in very small groups; it barely looks like a rhododendron at all.[58] Yet there are some characters in common: bilaterally symmetrical flowers, clusters of leaves representing each new year's growth, pods with large numbers of tiny seeds, and stringy pollen. These characters would therefore have been in the *Rhododendron* common ancestor, too.

DNA evidence also gives us a very rough idea of when major divergence events occurred. Around 40 million years ago, three major lineages diverged: subgenus *Rhododendron* (the 'lepidotes'), *Hymenanthes* plus *Pentanthera*, and *Tsutsusi*.[59] All three lineages are predominantly Asian, so the divergence event probably happened there. The relationships of some of the eclectic oddments within *Rhododendron*, such as *Menziesia*, *R. albiflorum*, *R. semibarbatum* and the group including *R. schlippenbachii*, are not yet certain, but these may have diverged around this time, or soon after.

Sections *Pentanthera* and *Rhodora* of subgenus *Pentanthera* split from evergreen *Hymenanthes* around 22 million years ago.[60] Until about 5 million years ago, northeast Russia was connected to Alaska via the now submerged Bering Land Bridge. Conditions there would have been quite unlike anything on Earth today: mild (for the planet was

Rhododendron forrestii, a beautiful dwarf species named after its discoverer, George Forrest.

Enkianthus chinensis, a living plant that resembles the common ancestor of the family Ericaceae, from 90 million years ago.

far warmer), but completely dark in winter, because it lay within the Arctic Circle.[61] These conditions might have driven the evolution of a deciduous habit in *Pentanthera* as it moved across the bridge into North America.

The subgenus *Hymenanthes* began to diversify about 10 million years ago, beginning with the *Pontica* group, whose ten or eleven species appear to have diverged from one another before retreating to their current locations in North America, the Black Sea region and northeast Asia.[62] At least one lineage from this group moved to western China or thereabouts, where it was profoundly affected by the uplift of the massive Tibetan Plateau, an after-effect of the collision between India and Asia.[63] This helped the Himalayas attain their modern, monstrous size. As the land rose, erosion increased, creating massive river valleys like the three that cut through Yunnan. Habitats in the region changed rapidly, and plants evolved fast to keep pace. Every patch of ground had different conditions, depending on altitude, slope, aspect and rain shadows. Rhododendron populations became separated by giant ridges and valleys, each population evolved independently of others, and so within a few million years, *Hymenanthes* exploded into more than 200 distinct species.[64] The same happened to subgenus *Rhododendron*, which also diversified into hundreds of species in the region. This evolution is certainly still ongoing, as evidenced by geographical variation within so many species, noticed by Forrest:

> I have really given up on attempting to define the limits of a species; each individual seems to have a form, or an affinity, on every range and divide, differing essentially from the type.[65]

Remarkably, hybridization may have accelerated the evolution process. A group of Chinese *Rhododendron* species, comprising *asterochnoum*, *calophytum*, *insigne*, *praevernum* and *sutchuenense*, all bear a genetic marker from a now extinct *Pontica* species, suggesting that they may have originated from ancient hybridization between distantly related evolutionary lines.[66] Hybridization creates novelty, as generations of nurserymen have demonstrated, and in the right conditions can very rapidly produce new species. For example, *R. balangense* might have

Rhododendron camtschaticum, the Rhododendron least like any other.

evolved from hybrids between R. *watsonii* and R. *prattii*.[67] Tantalizingly, disagreement between *Rhododendron* evolutionary trees based on different genetic markers might indicate that hybridization events deep in the history of *Rhododendron* may have accelerated the evolution of the genus.

The careers of many great collectors span one decade, or sometimes two. Frank Kingdon-Ward is exceptional in that his numerous collecting trips spanned 48 years, and that the only breaks of over a year between any of them were to serve in the world wars.[68] Exploring was his passion; collecting was how he paid the wages while he did it. He spent two years as a teacher in China as soon as he finished his degree, but quit the job at the first opportunity to join an expedition, in 1909. A year later Bulley engaged him as a plant collector, sending him to Yunnan. Throughout his career, Ward collected alone or with few companions, reflecting his adventurous spirit.[69]

Kingdon-Ward had two weaknesses: a morbid fear of heights, and an almost comical absence of any sense of direction. Several times he got completely lost, often having left the path on his own to hunt plants. On one such occasion he had to stave off hunger by eating rhododendron flowers, suffering mild poisoning as a consequence. Yet set against this was an incredibly accurate memory for the locations of plants, which served him extremely well when, for example, he needed to gather seeds months later from some beauty he had seen in flower. He was also luckier than many, although he endured his fair share of health problems early on. He survived several falls off cliffs, and one occasion when a house collapsed on top of him.[70]

Kingdon-Ward discovered or introduced 100 *Rhododendron* species, all of which (unlike Forrest) he saw at first hand.[71] He described, for example, the excitement of his discovery of R. *cinnabarinum* ssp. *xanthocodon* with orange flowers, 'that rarest of all colours', on a barely accessible cliff face. He personally returned to gather its seeds in the late autumn, fighting through snow to get it.[72]

Rhododendron praevernum, a species whose DNA shows a signature of ancient hybridization between two distantly related evolutionary lines.

Ward's most celebrated of expeditions was through the Tsangpo Gorges in Tibet and the northern tip of Arunachal Pradesh (northeast India). In 1924 these were unexplored, and supposedly full of deadly tribes and impossibly high waterfalls. It was suspected that the Tsangpo River of southern Tibet became the Brahmaputra of India and Bangladesh, but no one had ever successfully completed the journey from one to the other, so it remained unproven. Such a lure was irresistible to Kingdon-Ward's adventurous spirit, and he set out from Tibet on an expedition down the Tsangpo Gorges that plunged through the Himalayas. He reached the end of the Brahmaputra and found numerous new *Rhododendron* species along the way, including *venator*, *exasperatum*, *auritum* and *pemakoense*.[73] Among his later introductions would be the magnificent R. *macabeanum*.

Ward's first marriage ended after fourteen years, perhaps unsurprisingly as he was seldom at home. His second wife Jean had no such problems, because she accompanied him on his travels, and wrote her own book about them.[74] Together they survived the great Assam–Tibet

Rhododendron macabeanum, a dramatically beautiful species introduced to gardens by Frank Kingdon-Ward.

earthquake of 1950 (magnitude 8.6), although it 'ruined the harvest' of alpine plants.[75] He was still climbing great Asian mountains in his early seventies.[76]

During the 1930s Edinburgh Botanic Garden had begun inviting Chinese botanists over for formal training in Western science. Among these was Yü Te-Tsun, a renowned intellectual, plant collector and polymath, who brought with him seed of numerous rhododendrons, and who would later play a key role in initiating the Flora of China project.[77] Yü also co-founded the Kunming Institute of Botany, which would ultimately become a centre of rhododendron research in China, as well as Beijing Botanical Garden. Another guest, Wen Pei Fang, became the first Chinese expert on formal *Rhododendron* taxonomy,[78] but paid a heavy personal price for his time at Edinburgh, missing his beloved mother's funeral. He atoned by naming a *Rhododendron* after her.[79]

By 1950 these men had returned to China, with Fang promising to visit Britain again. Their goal now was to train others and establish modern plant science in China. Though they would eventually succeed, their timing was unfortunate, for then came the Chinese Civil War, and the triumph of Mao's communists. Joseph Rock, the last Western plant collector in China at the time, had to jump on a plane and flee.[80] Anti-intellectual tensions culminated in the Cultural Revolution, which saw scientific research halted and scientists sent to labour in the fields. At some point during these dark times, the faithful Wen Pei Fang had both his legs broken.[81]

After Mao's death, China transitioned to a more pragmatic communism, and Deng Xiaoping encouraged scientific endeavour to resume. Remembering their old friendships, Yü, Fang and others invited Western botanists to come to China, in 1980, making these some of the first Western scientists to set foot in China for thirty years. A regretful, limping Fang told them, 'You must realize that I am an old man now, and can no longer keep my promise to study again outside China.'[82] Instead, he recommended his brightest young protégé, Hu Chi-Ming, and collaboration resumed.

Kunming Botanical Garden, with one of the Kunming Institute of Botany's science buildings visible in the background. It is now a hotbed of research into *Rhododendron*.

The following year saw the first field excursion, yielding ample rhododendrons including hybrids between *decorum* and *delavayi*. Unlike past expeditions, the party was led by Chinese scientists, setting the pattern for future botanical excursions.[83] In other ways, the trip resembled earlier ones, with locals marvelling at the unfamiliar Caucasian faces, and cries of 'mah-wah!' ringing out to warn the party of leeches.[84]

More visits followed, with Chinese scientists viewing it as a great honour to participate, but they were plagued by an ever-present worry that harm might befall their 'exalted' visitors, such as when one ran with abandon down a long mountain scree slope. In 1989, however, a visiting expedition in Sichuan faced more serious peril, following the events in Tiananmen Square. Many westerners in Chengdu were hopping on flights to Kabul (for some reason the only ones available), but Hu Chi-Ming took his group to a home for retired Communist Party members, where they could lie low until things calmed down. This was no hardship, for it was an area of spectacular limestone cascades, and they saw the rare *R. rufum*. The biggest risk for modern plant hunters in China is on the roads, and on one occasion a group of botanists had to flee for their lives from their burning vehicle. On later trips, botanists crossed into Vietnam, watching large numbers of battered warplanes from each side patrolling the border.[85]

Throughout this period, the number of Chinese plant scientists was steadily growing, as men like Hu Chi-Ming and Wu Chengyi trained up new generations. More recently, while Western economies have struggled and funding for science has tightened, a booming China has spent copious amounts to generate world-class research programmes. At Kunming, Gao Lianming is leading the most comprehensive study yet of DNA relationships among rhododendrons,[86] and Chinese researchers collaborate with Europeans to unpick the secrets of giant hybrid populations like that at Baili.

In Chengdu, Mao Kangshan and Professor Liu Jianquan have initiated a project to add *R. ponticum* to the small but growing list of plants for which the complete DNA sequence is known, alongside rice

Rhododendron aganniphum (foreground) and *rufum* (background), in the Valley Gardens at Windsor Great Park.

and tobacco.[87] From this we may finally learn the exact effect that hybridization with R. *catawbiense* has had on the invasive British *ponticum* populations (see Chapter Eight), and answer big questions about rhododendron evolution. Once, the Chinese were mere extras in the story of their flora and its discovery. Now, at last, they have rightly taken centre stage.

six

Potions, Petals and Poisons
❀

Hast thou found honey? Eat only so much as is sufficient for thee,
lest thou be filled therewith, and vomit it.

KING JAMES BIBLE, PROVERBS 25:16

A legend from China tells how a shepherd brought his cows
up to graze in the cool grassy fields of the Baili area of
northwest Guizhou, in the spring when the rhododendrons were in bloom. Upon seeing the spectacular floral display, the
cows became intoxicated with the beauty of the place, and fell about
drunk. The tale is a gift to the local tourist board, who have erected
a life-sized statue of the inebriated bovines inside the reserve. There,
Chinese tourists now spew forth from their vehicles to photograph
the rhododendrons. There is, indeed, as least one *Rhododendron* species
that can cause effects like drunkenness merely by sniffing the flowers,[1]
but *Rhododendron tomentosum* does not grow at Baili. Instead, the legend
possibly stems from poisoning caused by cows eating *Rhododendron*
species that they had not learned to avoid. Rhododendrons are well
known to be poisoners of livestock in China.

Ornamental plants are a relatively recent development in human
history, whereas the chemical properties of rhododendrons have
affected human beings for far longer, poisoning animals but offering
medical treatments for a great breadth of ailments. Although all
rhododendrons are poisonous to varying degrees, some are occasionally used as food and drinks, but more often as intoxicants. They have

114

also been used in religious ceremonies, and for more mundane purposes like firewood, tools and construction. In both myth and reality, they have been weapons of war.

The year was 67 BC, and the mighty Roman Empire had been fighting King Mithradates VI of Pontus intermittently for 21 years. They had forced him into retreat, but could not win against a guerrilla war fought from the steep valleys and ridges of the Pontic Mountains. Consequently, the Roman commander Lucullus had been fired and replaced with Pompey the Great.[2]

Now, seeking the elusive Mithradates, 1,000 of Pompey's men passed through the territory of the Heptakometes, fearsome allies of Mithradates who originally lived in trees or portable wooden towers, around modern İkizdere.[3] These Romans encountered no resistance; instead, they found pots of delicious local honeycombs, apparently left behind as a tribute.[4] No one suspected foul play, and the soldiers scoffed the lot. It was a fatal mistake. Within four hours or less, they would have started to feel ill.[5] Soon they would be delirious,

Statue of the 'Drunken Cows' at a roadside stopping place at Baili, in China, commemorating the legend of animals supposedly intoxicated by the beauty of the local rhododendrons.

Ancient opponents: King Mithradates IV of Pontus (135–65 BC; left), and the Roman general Pompey the Great (106–28 BC).

hallucinating, vomiting or unconscious, and all certainly unable to defend themselves. The Heptakometes emerged from their hiding places and slaughtered them.[6]

It was to be one of the last victories for Mithradates. The following year Pompey finally trapped his army in a narrow ravine and inflicted a crushing defeat. Mithradates escaped, but was eventually betrayed by his son, and responded by taking his own life.[7]

Some two millennia later, a very experienced American horti-culturalist was trying to get a close-up shot of *Rhododendron* 'Lady Chamberlain' in Inverewe Garden in Scotland. A couple of drops of nectar happened to fall onto his finger, and he licked them off without thinking. He very soon realized he was in trouble, as pins and needles in his limbs gave way to partial paralysis. Separated from his companions, he somehow made it to a bench. Within five minutes he felt acute depression, soon accompanied by dread, disorientation and a feeling of floating helplessly in space. After twenty minutes he man-aged to stumble and stagger back to his group. Unable to form words correctly, he managed to explain that he had suffered 'doderendron' (sic) poisoning. He then felt extreme hunger and thirst, drowsiness and an intense headache, which eventually he was able to sleep off.[8] It was a rare British case of what the Turks call 'mad honey disease'.[9]

Stories of rhododendron honey poisoning are scattered throughout history. The first recorded cases occurred in 401 BC, when Xenophon led a returning Greek army of 10,000 through Colchis on the Black Sea coast. Having robbed the local bee colonies for honey, they were soon insensible – some violently inebriated, others unconscious – and 'a great despondency' fell upon them.[10] Yet the locals wisely left them well alone, and a few days later all had recovered enough to stagger on home.

Most parts of rhododendrons are rendered poisonous by a class of toxins called grayanotoxins, of which so-called andromedotoxins are a subgroup. Some, especially *Pentanthera* species, have grayanotoxins in their nectar. Symptoms of grayanotoxin poisoning include nausea, severe sweating, vomiting, dizziness and a drop in blood pressure.[11] Most reported incidents are from the Black Sea region, implicating *R. ponticum* and *R. luteum* as the main culprits. Both grow abundantly

Mountain slopes above İkizdere, the area where Pompey's troops succumbed to the honey trap set by Mithradates and the Heptakometes.

Kalmia angustifolia, known as 'spoonwood' or sheep laurel, an American plant that shares some uses with rhododendron and makes equally hazardous honey.

on mountain slopes south of the Black Sea, and locals know to be wary of raw honey made when they are in flower.[12]

Despite this, accidental poisonings still occur. A 56-year-old Turkish driver lost consciousness, causing a traffic accident, three hours after eating two tablespoons of wild honey, and in the spring of 2010, no fewer than 21 patients were admitted to an Istanbul hospital with grayanotoxin poisoning caused by honey.[13] Hooker mentions similar effects from honey in India, and recently in the USA a man from Seattle who had eaten raw honey suffered 'irregular heart beat, low blood pressure, loss of muscle control (including arms and bowels), numbness, extreme nausea and vomiting for 24 hours straight, and a costly visit to the ER'.[14] An early warning of having eaten 'mad' honey is a sharp burning sensation in the throat, and it is claimed that a tingling sensation can be felt when a drop is placed on the skin of one's hand.[15]

Grayanotoxins are widely distributed among the Ericaceae, but in the family, only *Rhododendron* and *Kalmia* seem to make enough toxic nectar to cause honey poisoning.[16] *Nerium oleander*, a Mediterranean plant much confused with *Rhododendron* in pre-Linnaean literature because both have been called 'rhododaphne', also has hallucinogenic honey. It may have been responsible for the visions of the Delphic oracles, but not the Pontus or Colchis poisonings, because it favours much drier regions.[17]

Apparently, the concentration and preservation process by the bees themselves eventually inactivates the toxins. Therefore Hooker was told by Nepalese locals that raw honey should be avoided when rhododendrons were in flower, but later in the year it would become safe.[18] The risk from raw honey varies dramatically between years, as variation in weather and flowering patterns determines how much nectar the bees take from rhododendrons.[19]

Plants use poisons to defend themselves, but petals are a short-lived organ barely worth protecting in this way, so the petals of some *Rhododendron* species may be eaten. In western China, ethnic Han, Bai and Yi people eat the petals of *R. decorum*, but only after boiling and/or soaking them in regularly changed water for several days, to

Soup made from the flowers of *Rhododendron decorum* in a restaurant in western China.

remove toxins. They are eaten in soups, stir-fries or with eggs, and served to tourists as local delicacies in restaurants in Yunnan.[20]

Rhododendron arboreum grows abundantly on the south side of the Himalayas, where the locals call it *burans*. Its flowers can be eaten raw in small quantities, but too many will cause intoxication, suggesting that they contain small amounts of grayanotoxins.[21] Nonetheless, Himalayan people eat them as salad vegetables when other food is scarce.[22] A safer culinary use, which probably destroys the toxins, is to pickle them, and some Nepalese do this using salt and chilli, while in Uttarakhand they are ground together with soaked tamarind, chillies and garlic to make chutney; they also make burans pakoras.[23]

Chutney is also made from flowers of *R. campanulatum*, and in Nepal the flowers of *R. anthopogon* are boiled and drunk as tea.[24] More recently, enterprising locals in Uttarakhand have begun making a squash-type drink from *R. arboreum* flowers, cunningly marketing it as an unofficial state drink, based on its recent adoption as the state flower.[25] Wine is also made from the flowers in both Nepal and India.[26] Even the leaves of *R. arboreum* are supposedly occasionally eaten as vegetables, though only in their youngest, most tender state, and possibly only in very lean times.[27] Remarkably, even the petals of the otherwise highly toxic *R. cinnabarinum* find their way onto the dinner table, for some Indians make jam from them.[28] This must be done with care, for *Rhododendron* 'Lady Chamberlain' is derived mainly from this species, and if even a drop of nectar passes the mouth it will bring 'mad honey disease'.

In some rhododendrons, however, even the petals are toxic. *R. mucronulatum* causes occasional poisoning events in South Korea, where some people erroneously think its flowers are good to eat.[29] Another Korean man was so desperately thirsty that he ate fifty flowers of *R. schlippenbachii*, in this case knowing but perhaps underestimating the consequences.[30] The great explorer Kingdon-Ward once ate rhododendron flowers out of desperation on one of several occasions when he got a bit lost, and paid for it with a stomach ache.[31] However, among 152 cases of Americans (mainly children) who had eaten *Rhododendron*, only fourteen required treatment, and just one was

Indian women making Buransh drink from *Rhododendron arboreum* flowers.

hospitalized with hypertension.[32] Other than by nectar or honey, it
is hard to consume enough *Rhododendron* to do oneself significant
harm. Nonetheless, campers in the USA who roast marshmallows or
'smores' on the fire using *Rhododendron* twigs often get stomach aches,
and a few can get allergic reactions from the juice of the plant, or
more rarely a skin rash just from brushing past the flowers.[33]

While most human poisonings come from honey, livestock poisonings are caused by eating the leaves. Limb paralysis, briefly experienced
by the horticulturalist at Inverewe, is more severe and prolonged in
animal poisonings, and untreated animals suffering paralysis usually
die.[34] Chinese vernacular names like 'sheep staggers' (see Introduction)
refer to this effect. Cattle can be killed by eating 0.2 per cent of their
body weight in rhododendron leaves;[35] sheep and goat poisonings
are equally common, but these have a greater chance of recovery. Cats
and dogs are occasionally poisoned by eating or chewing garden
rhododendrons, but deer in North America can apparently eat rhododendrons with impunity, due to an enzyme in their stomachs.[36]

The very rare R. *afghanicum* is reputedly highly poisonous, and local
nomads in Kurrum Valley in Afghanistan took care to prevent their
sheep from eating the plant.[37] In Britain, the only cultivated plants

Rhododendron mucronulatum: unlike some species, even the flowers are poisonous.

of it were deliberately destroyed in the late 1940s, for fear that they would poison livestock, though it was eventually reintroduced.[38]

Animals with no natural experience of rhododendrons may not know to avoid them, which might explain poisonings of kangaroos, alpacas, llamas and Brazilian goats.[39] Even in Britain, when thirty young sheep were moved to a new pasture that contained *R. ponticum*, half of them nibbled or ate it, and suffered varying degrees of poisoning; two died.[40] Poisonings also occur when sheep escape from fields and get the chance to sample unfamiliar plants, or when clippings are carelessly left where animals can get them.[41]

In Scotland, however, both *R. ponticum* and sheep run free in the hills, and sheep seem to learn not to eat rhododendron. Nonetheless, poisonings do sometimes occur during heavy winter snow cover, when no other food is available.[42] All is not lost, however, if a poisoned sheep or goat is found in time, for a remarkable antidote exists: tea! This knowledge is passed among farmers, vets and shepherds in Britain.[43] Strong black tea is brewed in a large pot, cooled and then administered by bottle, or even a drinking tube into the stomach if the animal is in a bad way. Sometimes this is combined with bicarbonate of soda

A sheep and its lamb, in a field where *Rhododendron ponticum* is within easy reach. These animals have clearly learned not to eat the plant, though they may try if no other food is available.

to bring up gas, and oil to line the stomach preventing any further absorption; either could be preceded by melted lard and soda as an emetic.[44]

Poisons can also be useful. Leaves of R. *arboreum* are among plants used to incapacitate fish by fishermen in Nepal and elsewhere, and their juice is used to repel bugs from bedding by the Doti people of Nepal.[45] In Bhutan, R. *thomsonii* is used as an insecticide.[46] *Rhododendron tomentosum* was traditionally used against mice, bedbugs, fleas and lice in the Baltic and Scandinavian countries,[47] and extracts from it have been shown to be highly effective as repellents for mosquitoes, ticks and pests of stored food. It is now used in commercial mosquito repellents in Italy.[48]

Rhododendron molle also has a long history of local use as an insecticide, effective enough to make it economically viable for local people to dry and pulverize flowers from the wild plant for sale in Chinese drug stores.[49] It is effective in the extermination of many plant-eating insect pests, including the famous Colorado potato beetle, *Leptinotarsa decemlineata*, and the diamondback moth, *Plutella xylostella*, regarded as the world's worst pest of brassicaceous plants.[50] The toxin interferes with feeding and larval development, and helpfully deters insects from laying eggs on treated plants. As pests develop resistance to synthetic insecticides, this compound could acquire major economic importance.

The sheer abundance of rhododendrons in general, and R. *arboreum* in particular, invites simpler uses around the Himalayas. *Rhododendron hodgsonii* is used for basket lining, and the leaves of this and R. *kesangiae* are used to pack butter and cheese in Bhutan. Traditional Bhutanese bowls called dapa are made from rhododendron wood, while the wood of species such as R. *hodgsonii*, R. *arboreum* and R. *falconeri* is used to make implements both small and large, including crockery, spoons and yak saddles.[51] Various Chinese ethnic groups do likewise, and Tibetans make an even wider range of objects, including yak butter churners.[52] Native Americans in California harvested abalone shellfish using a spatula made from hardened wood of R. *occidentale*.[53]

Rhododendron molle, one of the most toxic Chinese species, is being called into service as an insecticide.

The wood of large Himalayan rhododendrons is used in building, although wood of *R. arboreum* tends to warp, so where possible *R. falconeri* is preferred. As a fuel source they are far too abundant to be ignored, but smoke from both *R. campanulatum* and *R. cinnabarinum* is said to be acrid and to cause irritation of the eyes, and there is plenty of it because the wood smoulders, as Joseph Hooker experienced on his travels.[54]

Yet smoke can be desirable in context. A wide range of *Rhododendron* species, including *anthopogon*, *nivale*, *fragariiflorum*, *setosum* and *lepidotum*, are mixed with juniper berries in Bhutan to make incense.[55] Buddhist temples are often decorated by flowers of *R. arboreum*.[56] In the USA, rhododendrons are the subject of a week-long festival at Kitsap in Washington, whereas Kashaya and Pomo Native Americans bedeck themselves in *R. macrophyllum* flowers to dance at their Strawberry Festival to celebrate spring.[57]

Rhododendrons play an unusually prominent role in the Dongba belief system of the Naxi people of northern Yunnan, which captured the imagination of collector Joseph Rock. Dongba rituals are based around creation myths, and these are preserved in handwritten books. Each new book produced is a retelling rather than a copy, allowing the stories to evolve like an orally transmitted tradition.[58] In general, Chinese mythology links the rhododendron to tragedy, dead souls and the cuckoo (see Chapter Seven), but here they are bound up with war and conflict.

Dongba tales describe the creation of Dongba people, their world and its inhabitants, both real and mythical. The rhododendrons in these stories fall into three distinct kinds, which, thanks to Joseph Rock, we know the identities of. Most significant in the tales was the 'black' rhododendron or *munna*, which was *R. decorum*, with its very dark bark. The 'white' rhododendron or *shwua* referred to *R. rubiginosum* or the related *heliolepis*, whereas 'great rhododendron' or *munlua* was the larger *R. adenogynum* or any superficially similar species.[59]

Their world began when the heroic Ddù landed on Shílo Mountain and fought epic battles with the monstrous, evil Ssù. Rhododendrons are scattered across these blood-soaked legends: the warriors carried sword sheathes made from the black rhododendron, and their shields and armour were cut from the great rhododendron. In one tale, soldiers are commanded to carve 10,000 suits of armour and shields from just three plants of it. Ssù commanded an army including legions of ghosts, yet eventually he was defeated, slain and dismembered. Ddù's army scattered Ssù's body parts across the landscape, but every piece brought conflict where it fell: bird fought bird, beast fought beast, and soldiers fought against their own weapons. When a piece was placed among black rhododendrons on a hilltop, 10,000 sword sheaths sprang forth from the plants to fight one another.[60]

During Dongba rituals, relevant legends are read aloud. At spiritual cleansing ceremonies for bodies or dwellings, torches called *soshwua* are used. Legend tells how the son of Ddù shot and cremated the son of Ssù, and the resulting clouds of smoke turned into the black rhododendron, the white rhododendron and the dragon spruce. Five branches then emerged from the mountain and fought with these purifying torches. *Soshwua* torches may contain a range of trees and herbs, including white rhododendron, but always have a skin of black rhododendron.

Dongba belief allows objects such as plants, or things made from them, to acquire limited awareness and specific powers, and hence become part-beings, which can be used to battle spirits. Like *soshwua*, voodoo-like figures called *ngawbä* are constructed and imbued with life during rituals. At least twenty types of *ngawbä* could be created, each with different features and powers; these included Auntie Rhododendron Woman, whose hair was adorned with rhododendron twigs. Sometimes there was an Uncle Rhododendron Man, too. The fate of all these would depend on the ritual and which role they played; sometimes they would represent allies against demons, but if they represented enemies they could be beheaded and burnt.[61]

The three rhododendrons featured in Dongba legend: The 'Black' is *decorum* (left), the 'White' is either *rubiginosum* (top right) or *heliolepis* and the 'Great' is *adenogynum* (bottom right) or similar.

Dongba culture is said to have begun at Shílo Mountain, where its founder Ddibba landed with his sacred text. *Ngawbä* were supposedly fathered by three black rhododendrons that grew at its peak, which was the gateway between the land of the living and those of gods, monsters and the dead.[62] All human souls must pass that way when they die. For Dongba followers, *R. decorum* frames their beginning, and their end.

More light-hearted Naxi myths tell how the arrogant rhododendron was late to answer an invite from the Fairy Queen, and so lost the chance to sit beside her. Among Naxi, calling a girl 'rhododendron' means she is superficially pretty, but poisonous on the inside. Like Naxi, some Yi minority people in China use rhododendrons to cast out unwanted spirits from their homes. They also use rhododendron flowers to bless newly planted crops, and rhododendron leaves to bless hunters' kills. However, some believe that the plants can attract damaging spirits towards their children.[63]

As with so many poisonous plants, rhododendrons have been much used in herbal medicine. Such uses and knowledge are thinly spread among a wide range of ethnic groups in China, and seem more prominent in countries south of the Himalayas.[64] Grayanotoxins are known to lower blood pressure, for example – something that can in turn increase the human lifespan.[65] In the Himalayas, *R. arboreum* is used for an extraordinary range of health complaints, including diabetes and ailments of the heart, liver and skin, diarrhoea and dysentery, headaches and stomach ailments, wounds, nosebleeds, and even removing fish bones stuck in the throat.[66] These uses variously employ petals, infusions, juice, bark or chutneys. The bark is used to make a form of snuff, and leaves or a paste thereof are held on the head as a headache cure. The chutney described above is regularly eaten as a remedy for sickness associated with spring changes in the weather. *Rhododendron campanulatum* is used as a remedy for chronic rheumatism, syphilis and many of the same conditions as *R. arboreum*.[67] Both species are used in Bhutan to treat diarrhoea, dysentery, rheumatism and sciatica.[68]

In Nepal, wounds on cattle are treated using juice from young leaves of *R. dalhousiae*.[69]

Rhododendron anthopogon reportedly has stimulant properties.[70] It is used in Himachal Pradesh for throat and lung conditions, including coughs and colds, asthma, chronic bronchitis and lung infections, whereas if mixed with ghee, it makes a treatment for gonorrhoea and leucorrhoea. A massage oil mixed with leaves and flowers of the plant is used to treat new mothers with complications following birth.[71] The Nepalese make tea from it, and inhale vapour from boiled leaves to treat colds and throat conditions.[72] In Turkey, leaves of *R. ponticum* have long been used to make a diuretic.[73]

Needless to say, great care must be taken in the use of folk remedies, especially when they involve plants or substances known to be poisonous. The concentration of active ingredients is hard to control, and the outcome can be disastrous. Local people in the modern Pontic

Rhododendron campanulatum: after *R. arboreum*, the most used species by local people in India and Nepal.

Commercially
produced
rhododendron
tea from Nepal.

Mountains of Turkey, while aware of the dangers of mad honey, view
it as an alternative remedy for digestive disorders such as gastritis,
rheumatism, diabetes, a flagging sex drive, ulcers and hypertension,
but often the actual outcome is a trip to hospital.[74] An eight-year-old
boy in Trabzon suffered 'mad honey disease' in 2002, after his parents
deliberately gave him raw honey as a medicine.[75] Similarly, a baby in
Hong Kong became seriously ill after being given an extract of *R. simsii*
by its grandmother.[76] In Korea several people suffered poisoning after
taking medicines made from rhododendrons.[77] Paradoxically, most
of these were treated using atropine, which is derived from the even
more poisonous deadly nightshade, *Atropa belladonna*.

Perhaps the most broadly used rhododendrons, for their chemical
properties, are two widespread species from northern bogs: *R. tomentosum* and *R. groenlandicum*. These were previously classified as a separate
genus, *Ledum*, and only recently incorporated into *Rhododendron* (see
Chapter Two). Both species have been used as a diuretic, or to treat
respiratory complaints and skin problems, including leprosy.[78] *Rhododendron groenlandicum* is commonly used by native people in Canada to

make infusions, earning it the common name 'Labrador Tea'.[79] Native Americans use it to treat colds, burns, ulcers and rheumatism.[80]

In Europe, *R. tomentosum* is sometimes called wild, marsh or bog rosemary, the last a name more commonly applied to the related *Andromeda polifolia*. Tea from *R. tomentosum* was used in the past to treat asthma, heart disease, lung disease, diarrhoea, dysentery and forms of malaria.[81] In Estonia, reported uses extend to inducing abortions, curing horse coughs and treating red spot disease in pigs, or mixing it with horse dung in a soothing bath to treat rheumatism.[82] More recently, *R. tomentosum* has been commercialized as a cough medicine in both Russia and China. It helps protect the body from radiation, at least in mice, and the Chinese claim remarkable properties in aiding recovery from drug addiction.[83]

Rhododendron tomentosum contains such powerful volatile compounds that the mere scent of it can cause intoxication.[84] In Estonia, people know not to rest or sleep among the flowering plants. On one occasion, a lady did not return from collecting berries in an Estonian wood, and concerned neighbours eventually found her passed out among *R. tomentosum* the following morning.[85] Removed from their presence, she quickly recovered. Most intoxications from this plant, however, are deliberate.

The brewing of ales in Europe appears to have started around 4,000 years ago, with Scottish heather, but it was around 1,000 years ago that gruit-based ales became common. Gruit is a herbal mixture that normally included, but was not necessarily limited to, three species: yarrow (*Achillea millefolium*), bog myrtle or sweet gale (*Myrica gale*), and 'ledum' (*Rhododendron tomentosum* or *groenlandicum*). Ledum imparts a pleasantly bitter taste to beer, together with a narcotic effect, which is strongest in *R. tomentosum*. Between them, these plants supposedly greatly stimulated the mind, causing euphoria. Psychotic trips could occur, and sexual desire is heightened without (unlike with modern beers) dampening the performance.[86] The effect, therefore, was quite different from modern hop-based beers, and more like that of cannabis.

Rhododendron tomentosum population in a wooded bog, Estonia.

Brewing beer from R. *tomentosum* is potentially straightforward; one suggested recipe involves 115 g (4 oz) of the plant, 2.3 kg (5 lb) of malt, 455 g (1 oz) of brown sugar, 23 litres (5 gallons) of water, and yeast. With a suitable fermenter, the beer will be ready in two weeks. To get the greatest narcotic effect from the plant, brewers knew to take the fresh tips of flowering stems, in which active ingredients were most concentrated.[87] Overdoses are to be avoided, as these can lead to delirium, headaches and cramps, or even making the drinker go berserk.[88] One writer advised:

> Those who wanted drinkers to become stormy, sick, vomiting added Ledum [to their home brew]. This is not advised, because it takes reason from your head. Some fall down and vomit. Not everyone can take this.[89]

The three gruit herbs: *Rhododendron tomentosum* (left), bog myrtle (*Myrica gale*, top right) and yarrow (*Achillea millefolium*, bottom right).

R. tomentosum grew in quantity in Scandinavia and the Baltics down to parts of Germany, and is still common where bogs abound. It is absent from Britain, but populations of the American *R. groenlandicum* have grown for centuries on bogs in Stirlingshire.[90] These seem to have been artificially introduced, probably for beer production and/or for the many medical or insecticidal properties noted above.

The rise of Protestantism in Europe appears to have caused the decline of gruit ales. Protestants may have disapproved of the general merriment brought about by gruit ales, but what they really could not bear was all the money the Catholic Church was making by selling them.[91] Hence gruit ales were the very first casualty of the temperance movement, and their replacement by hop-based beers was encouraged. Indeed, the use of *R. tomentosum* in beer making was banned in Germany by 1855.[92] Perhaps, for the people in charge, a population rendered rowdy yet soporific on hoppy beer might be preferable to one enervated and encouraged to dream by its narcotic predecessors. Hops had largely taken over by 1750, but gruit ales went underground, surviving until the mid-twentieth century, in the hands of crafty home brew-makers in places where Church and State did not look too closely.[93]

seven

The Tears of the Cuckoo

He pointed to a low-walled enclosure . . . overlooked by two
large ginkgo trees and several rhododendron bushes that looked
as though they were discussing invasion plans.

JASPER FFORDE, *Shades of Grey* (2009)

The Yi people of southwest China have a flower god, whose symbol is carved onto the rock face in Baili, a sort of botanical equivalent of the Hollywood sign. For the Yi, the blood-red flowers of *R. delavayi* are a symbol of happiness and good luck, given by young men to express affection, and celebrated every year with a sumptuous dance festival. In these parts of China, rhododendrons are woven into the cultural landscape as deeply as the roots of the plants penetrate the mountain soil.

Some narrative themes are universal across cultures, such as tragedy, doomed love and their connection to nature. In a well-known Chinese children's song, a young woman sits alone on a hillside, looking sadly at the azaleas she and her lover had admired together the previous year, before he was swallowed up by a war.[1]

Blood, rhododendrons and cuckoos are interwoven in Chinese folklore, and ninth-century Chinese poems tell of cuckoos crying when the rhododendron flowers began to fall.[2] Often in stories, the bird is a transformed human soul, and it always sings with regret; usually the songs are accompanied by blood from its mouth or its eyes, from which spring the red rhododendrons. Most stories seem

A huge symbol of the Yi flower god carved into a cliff face in the Baili Azalea nature reserve, Guizhou, China.

to refer to the common, red-flowered *R. delavayi*, whose flowers are visited by birds, reinforcing the legends. One ancient story tells of a woman whose husband was conscripted straight after their marriage, condemning her to wait fruitlessly for his return. Worn down by this lonely vigil, she transformed into a cuckoo, from whose blood-soaked tears grew red azaleas.[3]

A Yi legend from Baili describes how two sisters died young from overwork, but their souls were unwilling to leave the land because of their love of rhododendrons, and turned into cuckoos. Eventually these, too, died from exhaustion, after singing every day and crying blood. They in turn transformed into two rocks whose shape is reminiscent of cuckoos, which have guarded the land ever since. Another Baili legend tells of a cuckoo pair separated by a great storm. The

Statue of the Rhododendron Woman, in the Baili Azalea nature reserve, Guizhou, China.

male then searched in vain for his lover for the rest of his days, calling always without reply. Eventually he succumbed to grief and exhaustion and fell among the rhododendrons, his blood dyeing them bright red.[4]

Every year on 8 February, the Yi people celebrate the Mayin Hua (a local name for *R. delavayi*) festival. They don colourful clothes, sing around the bonfire, and festoon their doors and the horns of their livestock with rhododendron flowers. The festival recalls the sacrifice of a beautiful young woman called Miyulu, who according to legend was coerced into the clutches of a corrupt local official who preyed on young women. She came to him wearing a white rhododendron flower in her hair, and used the flower to poison the wine which they both drank, living just long enough to see her tormentor die. Later, her heartbroken lover Zhaolieruo bore Miyulu's lifeless form across the mountains, and his grief turned his tears into blood. This blood stained white rhododendron flowers bright red, and they remain this colour in Miyulu's memory.[5] In fact, the flower of *delavayi* is barely poisonous, but perhaps the legend conflates it with other, more toxic species like *simsii*. The Nu minority in Yunnan also have a festival involving rhododendrons, celebrating A-Rong, a woman who designed rope bridges but was hounded to her death by a neighbouring chief.[6]

In another story, the farmer Liu Hu befriended the birds through his beautiful panpipe music, and fell in love with a girl called Juanzia (the name means azalea), who sang so beautifully that her voice opened the flowers on the mountain. When Juanzia was forcibly brought to the king to be his concubine, she refused to eat and disobeyed every order, determined to die rather than submit. Liu Hu set out on an epic journey to save her, but was unable to penetrate the palace. From outside, he played his pipe and she sang back to him. Eventually, in desperation, he transformed into a bird, and she into a red azalea, and so at last he could reach her and bear her away. Later a temple called Helin was erected in their honour, and the most beautiful of the azaleas that grow around it descend from Juanzia, while the bird that sings there like a panpipe comes from Liu Hu.[7]

Rhododendron delavayi, overlooking a karst landscape in the Baili Azalea nature reserve, Guizhou, China.

The Yi minority's Baili flower festival, which specifically celebrates rhododendrons, especially *R. delavayi* and its hybrids.

Equally tragic is the tale of two orphaned sisters, who are kidnapped one after the other by an evil landlord, and jump to their deaths to escape him. One becomes a cuckoo, whose song recalls the tragedy, and from whose mouth spilled blood from which grew rhododendrons.[8] The sex-crazed villains from these last three stories are all too realistic, more suited to gritty modern TV drama than Western folklore. Indeed, Western fairy tales paradoxically reassure children with monsters from outside the realm of humanity, but these Chinese tales make clear that the true monsters are, and have always been, human.

The folk tale connection between cuckoos (*Cuculus* species) and rhododendrons is upheld in their Chinese names: the bird is called 'Dujuan' and the rhododendron 'Dujuan Hua', or 'cuckoo flower'. Both supposedly get their names from a good, caring king called Duyu, who ruled the Sichuan area around the third century BC. There had been a time of terrible floods causing much suffering among Duyu's people, and only the dam-building deeds of his capable minister

Bieling had averted disaster. Tormented by thoughts of those he could not save, Duyu abdicated and quietly took himself into exile in the mountains outside of his country, leaving Bieling in charge. However, Duyu's longing for his country and his people grew stronger and stronger, until finally he sickened from it and died.[9]

Other versions attribute Duyu's shame to an affair with Bieling's wife, or have Duyu drop from exhaustion after forever walking through his country urging all he met to sow seed punctually.[10] In yet another, a spirit saves the king and his people from the flood, and Du Juan (or Duyu) remains king until his death.[11] In all versions, the dead king's soul passes into the Dujuan bird, giving it its name, and blood spilled from his mouth as he sung either created the rhododendron flowers or turned them red. The mournful song of the bird is said to be the voice of his soul, and its cry means either 'go home' or 'sow seed', depending on the version.[12]

Bird pollination in *Rhododendron delavayi*, in the wild in China.

Rhododendron simsii growing on a roadside in China.

The part of the story about Duyu abdicating in favour of Bieling is generally held to be true, though the individuals may represent dynasties, especially as Bieling had earlier supposedly undergone resurrection.[13] Duyu's story is referenced by the characters in the play *Qui Hu Tries to Seduce his Own Wife* by Shi Junbao (1279–1368), with a cuckoo urging the faithless husband to hasten home.[14]

Other Chinese stories concern brothers. One tells of a wicked mother who bullied and mistreated her older stepson while cosseting his younger half-brother. Eventually, her behaviour made the younger son run away. The elder son searched and searched for him fruitlessly, until the gods transformed him into a cuckoo, to aid his search. Yet still he searched in vain, eventually crying until his tears turned to blood, thus seeding the rhododendron.[15]

In an even sadder tale, the strong Du Da accidentally causes the death of a child, and is sentenced to death. His delicate younger brother, Du Er, fears that his family will starve without the strength of Du Da, and takes his place in prison. Du Er was duly executed, and his soul became a cuckoo, from whose blood-soaked tears grew the red rhododendron. Yet Du Da fled, racked with fear and guilt, leaving his parents uncared for. He died in the hills, and from that spot sprang the yellow-flowered Naoyanghua (*R. molle*), bringing madness to the goats that eat it.[16] The very real poisonous properties of this species supposedly derive from Du Da's cowardice, and several children's rhymes refer to this story.

A similar tale from southeast China tells how a young man called Du Juan offered to take the place of his condemned friend Xie Bao in prison for one afternoon, to give his friend one last taste of freedom. But Xie Bao fled, leaving Du Juan to be executed. Like Du Er's, his soul became a bird, and as he searched for the treacherous Xie Bao, he spat blood from which grew the red azalea.[17]

The theme of blood colouring plants appears in younger legends on the other side of the world, and again may be universal. In 1637 the Native American Pequot people were slaughtered by colonial forces in Cuppacommock, eastern Connecticut. Before he died, their leader Puttaquapouck supposedly declared that the golden hearts of the rhododendrons there 'would turn to blood as a perpetual reproach'.[18] Modern Pequot people commemorate this with rhododendron-themed plantings and stained-glass artwork around the Foxwoods Casino.[19]

In Nepalese legends, *Rhododendron arboreum* is a female who admired the strong, upright stature of the alder tree. She asked him to marry her, but he refused, scoffing at her scraggly branches and bent stems, and calling her ugly and ill-mannered for daring to court him. Undaunted, the rhododendron went about her business, and soon exploded into bloom. Upon seeing this, the regretful alder asked if she would forgive his rudeness, and marry him. She refused, for he had shown her his true nature. The lovesick alder threw himself into a steep gorge in suicidal despair, and that is where Nepalese alders are found to this day.[20]

In Western literature, rhododendrons tend to lurk at the fringes, playing the role of the often sinister outsider, most famously in Daphne du Maurier's classic *Rebecca*. On the very first page the nameless narrator returns in a dream to the ruins of Manderley, a place she had never been given the chance to enjoy, haunted as it was by memories of her predecessor, Rebecca. In the dream, the plants of the once well-manicured gardens had gone wild, and the rhododendrons 'stood fifty feet high, twisted and entwined with bracken, and they had entered into an alien marriage with a host of nameless shrubs'.[21]

Throughout the book, red rhododendrons provide one of the inescapable links to Rebecca. When the narrator first arrives at Manderley, her new husband asks her if she likes the 'blood-red' rhododendrons. She says yes, but does so

a little breathlessly, uncertain whether I was speaking the truth or not, for to me a rhododendron was a homely, domestic thing, strictly conventional, mauve or pink in colour, standing one beside the other in a neat round bed. And these were monsters, rearing to the sky, massed like a battalion, too beautiful I thought, too powerful; they were not plants at all.[22]

This contrast in her perception of different rhododendrons encapsulates perfectly the difference between how the narrator sees herself, and how she comes to see Rebecca. Curiously, Rebecca's influence has barely surfaced at this point, so this passage implies, perhaps, that it is in the narrator's nature to be overawed, unwittingly inviting the troubles that are to come.

The terms 'blood-red' and 'massed' turn up repeatedly to describe the rhododendrons lurking outside the house. In one particular room, the narrator notices that the rhododendrons, 'not content with forming their little theatre on the little lawn outside the window, had been permitted into the room itself', as if claiming this room above all others for the ghost of Rebecca.[23]

Initially at least, rhododendrons of other hues take a different role, as in 'Happy Valley', which is full of:

azaleas and rhododendrons, not blood-coloured like the giants in the drive, but salmon, white, and gold, things of beauty and grace, drooping their lovely, delicate heads in the soft summer rain.[24]

Gradually, however, Rebecca would claim even these for her own. Rebecca's perfume is described as smelling of white azalea, and the narrator later encounters that exact scent herself, as she fingers her predecessor's satin nightdress. Finally, her husband tells the narrator how the azaleas in Happy Valley had been down to Rebecca's 'blasted taste'.[25] Had the couple been given the chance to live longer at Manderley, it is hard to imagine that any of the rhododendrons or azaleas would have been allowed to continue growing there.

The word 'azalea' turns up far more often than 'rhododendron' in the titles of literary works, and even music. Perhaps this is due to

A huge blood-red rhododendron of the kind described in *Rebecca*, growing not at Caerhays but at Heligan.

Publicity poster for
Azalea Path, a play
about Sylvia Plath
written and directed
by Jack Wernick.

the sound of the words: Iggy Azalea works as a name for a female pop star; 'Iggy Rhododendron' not so much. Bing Crosby sung 'When the White Azaleas Start Blooming', while Europe frontman Joey Tempest, not content with inflicting 'The Final Countdown' on the world, produced a solo album called *Azalea Place*. In contrast, 'Rhododendrons' can only lay claim to being the title of an obscure (though rather interesting) song by the band Bloc Party, wherein the singer lies drunk among the plants at night, hiding from the expectations placed upon him.

'Azalea' appears in a few book titles, often reflecting the name of the lead character, as in Clayton Cecil's *Azalea* (1876). *The Rhododendron Man* (1930), by contrast, is the alias of a murderer in a detective story by Tyson Aubrey. The name of Frances Nugent's *The Azalea Garden* (2012) refers to the place where two thirteen-year-old girls first become friends, and in old age reunite to try and rescue some joy from their unhappy lives. *Rhododendron Pie* (1930) by Margery Sharp tells of a woman who rebels against her high-minded family, with a wish to be simple and conventional.

Sylvia Plath's poem 'Electra on Azalea Path' also refers to a place, rather than the plant, specifically the graveyard in which Plath's father Otto is buried.[26] By the time he died, when she was just eight, she had built up a visceral fury towards him, mixed with longing and an inability to break free of his hold; this all spewed forth in her 1962 poem 'Daddy'.[27] Even the FBI took an interest in Plath's father, because of his open support for Hitler's Nazis, although they couldn't prove anything except that he was a rather unpleasant man to know.[28]

Sylvia did not visit her father's grave in Azalea Path until nineteen years later, a moment which brought forth 'Electra on Azalea Path'. The names of both the poem and the graveyard contrast with their contents, for the only flowers in either are plastic: 'no flower breaks the soil', while an artificial sage drips 'a bloody dye' from its 'ersatz petals'.[29] Perhaps they are meant to cast a suggestion of travesty over her own incompatible longings, recalling the mythical Electra. A recent play called *Azalea Path* imagines the ghost of Sylvia returning to her father's grave, where she faces both family members and her own creative legacy.[30]

A graveyard is also the scene of Tim Bowling's poem 'The Rhododendron'. Like *Electra*, it is a meditation on death, but not just of a person – it seems to be about how all things must die, including childhood. It begins:

> Childhood has its own grave, and mine
> is tombed by the purple rhododendron
> blooming again in my mother's garden.[31]

Echoing 'Electra on Azalea Path', Anchee Min's *Red Azalea* (1993) is about a young woman dominated by a distant man with rigid political beliefs: Chairman Mao. The book describes the autumn days of Mao's China, through the eyes of its young heroine. In an emotionally complex story, she is offered an escape from despair and drudgery via possible stardom in the titular film, *Red Azalea*, a propaganda piece written by Madame Mao. Here, the red azalea ultimately represents communism. The same can be said of the title of Kenneth Ore's memoir, *Song of the Azalea* (2013), which tells of his young life in China and Hong Kong in the mid-twentieth century.

In Wee Kiat's *Azalea Dreams, Bamboo Lives* (2013), the flower again represents China, but in a more hopeful way. Launching her book, Kiat described how touched she was by the inscriptions on the Malayan graves of Chinese immigrants, all of whom chose to mention their place of origin on their epitaph. The titular azalea refers to the hopeful plans Kiat's characters had hatched, back in their Chinese homeland, only to have them checked by the 'bamboo' of the reality they encountered when attempting to forge new lives abroad.[32]

Rhododendron bushes, especially the ubiquitous *R. ponticum* in Britain, provide natural places for children to hide, as reflected in the title of Arthur Marshall's public school anthology *Whimpering in the Rhododendrons* (1982). Any adults trying to extract them would probably emerge muddy and empty-handed. When densely packed, rhododendrons form perfect adventure playgrounds, providing exciting climbing frames that are seldom so tall as to terrify any watching parents. The plethora of spreading branches form aerial highways for excited children to explore. Climbers can test out enigmatic masses of leaves and twigs to see if they can be stood on, and then call for rescue if they cannot. Underneath all this is a hidden maze of low curving tunnels, with carpets of slowly decaying leaves and ephemeral floral confetti, for kids to dart or crawl through, or simply play house. In *Light & Dark* (2000) by Margaret Thomson Davis, a girl plays hide and seek in the rhododendrons with a favourite servant, and they later use the plants to get back into the house unobserved. In Edith Nesbit's *The Railway Children* (1906), a girl pokes her head out of rhododendron leaves, and announces that her body parts are now widely distributed across the local area – something the others are happy to accept, in the way that only children can.

A 'tunnel' through an old copse of *Rhododendron ponticum* at Spanker's Hill Wood, Richmond Park, where children often play.

In Yaba Badoe's *True Murder* (2009), a schoolgirl goes exploring and finds:

> this secret place, a womb-like shelter between two [rhodo-dendron] bushes, roofed by intertwining tendrils in flower. Petals of dying rhododendron blooms littered the ground like tired balloons at the end of a party.[33]

The other children call this rhododendron patch 'Bouncy Town', implying that it is also a site of more vigorous games. The narrator, however, is coerced into playing a game of pretend murder among the rhododendrons, which goes terribly wrong. Milder injuries befall a boy who skateboards at high speed into a rhododendron bush in *The Bloodwater Mysteries: Doppelganger*. 'Um, it wasn't really the bush's fault,' he says, when a policeman asks if he has come to lodge a complaint against it.[34]

Rhododendrons turn up regularly in the murder mystery genre. According to *Murder on the Menu*,

> There is no sense in having a murder without a healthy stand of rhododendron, and no sense having a gardener other than to fight with Her Ladyship about them. Keeps everyone, including the rhododendron, in trim.[35]

Rhododendrons lurk passively in the background of no less than eight books by Ruth Rendell, including her debut *From Doon with Death* (1964), which echoes *Rebecca* with rhododendron flowers being 'massed' in a vase. In Rosella Rhine's light-hearted *Murder by Wheelchair*, the plants are the very scene of the crime:

English printed cotton by Hindleys, 1845–65, featuring rhododendrons, with two distinct colour forms present.

Dick, I hate to be the bearer of bad news, but Mrs Wilson, the southern lady from the second floor, is dead. I just found her wheelchair stuck in the middle of the rhododendron bushes with her head smashed like a dropped watermelon.[36]

The ITV adaptation of Agatha Christie's *Murder on the Links*, from 2011, sees the first body discovered when Captain Hastings hits a wayward golf ball into the flowering *R. ponticum* that lurk beyond the rough. In a 2012 *Lewis* episode called 'The Soul of Genius', a buried body is discovered by a party of conservationists tasked with digging up invasive *R. ponticum*, although the plant on screen is clearly not this species. The production team probably had to substitute another species, because planting *ponticum* in the wild is illegal.[37]

One real-life murder victim who had the grave misfortune to turn up dead in a rhododendron thicket was Doreen Marshall, in 1946. She had been the second victim of Neville Heath, a suave conman with a penchant for sexual sadism, whose charming exterior could not save him from hanging later that year.[38] In the 1990s the rhododendron expert David Chamberlain was called to act as an expert witness in a murder case. Newly developed forensic techniques allow pollen from individual rhododendron plants to be distinguished from one another, and police hoped this would place the prime suspect within metres of where the victim's body was found, in a public park. Upon his arrival at the scene, Dr Chamberlain had to inform the dismayed officers that the plants in question were not rhododendrons but cherry laurels.[39]

In fiction, the toxic properties of rhododendrons are occasionally used to attempt murder, as in *Murder on a Summer's Day* and *Lost Souls*.[40] Then there is Guy Ritchie's movie version of Sherlock Holmes, starring Robert Downey Jr, where a character fakes death by creating an 'apparently mortal paralysis' using 'a toxin refined from the nectar of the *Rhododendron ponticum*'. Holmes calls the effect 'mad honey disease', and demonstrates it using a dog who had 'seen far worse'. It's an enticing possibility, given that the poison does lower blood pressure, creating partial paralysis in animals, but neither full paralysis nor the near-cessation of pulse are among the recorded human symptoms of grayanotoxin poisonings (see Chapter Six), and it seems doubtful that 'refining' could bring forth such an effect.

Two books have gazed far into our future and found rhododendrons there. When H. G. Wells wrote *The Time Machine* in 1895, *R. ponticum* had not yet broken free from the shackles of cultivation, and when the book's narrator first arrives into the far future, he finds himself in a well-manicured garden, surrounded by rhododendron bushes. They, like all of nature, had been completely tamed.

More than a century later, Jasper Fforde's *Shades of Grey* (2009) depicts a strange, arbitrarily ordered human society greatly reduced in range and number, clinging on in towns surrounded by great swathes of countryside, which harbours deadly perils and is overrun with invasive rhododendrons. The species involved is never named, but to those in the know it is clearly *R. ponticum*, while to anyone else it wouldn't matter. Fforde, unlike Wells, had seen the twentieth century advance of this species through the British countryside, and simply extrapolated.

Oddly, *R. ponticum* is rather tame next to the numerous fictional organisms that populate the pages of *Shades of Grey*. There are bouncing goats, killer swans, ground sloths and man-eating trees called yateveos. Rhododendrons have gone from being alien interlopers of today to something relatively familiar, though still sinister. They provide one of the links to the past, representing the fall of the world that existed before, and the retreat of humanity. One of the book's many strengths is that as well as the very strange human society depicted, we witness the remnants not only of the world we live in, but of another far more advanced society that existed in between, before eventually imploding. Neither, apparently, had succeeded in eradicating *R. ponticum* from the countryside.

Eastern tales, therefore, concern the origins of rhododendrons, as befits plants that were there long before people, and represent their strong association with the place. In Western stories, the plants often

Rhododendron ponticum bushes near Inveraray, Scotland, that look as if they might be discussing plans for an invasion, as described in Jasper Fforde's *Shades of Grey* (2009).

bear witness to human affairs, only occasionally getting involved. When they do, all sides of them are on display: beauty and killer, manicured pet and rampant invader. Unlike in Eastern fiction, the plants often ground the story in reality, even in the strange futures imagined by Wells and Fforde.

eight
Black Sheep:
The Tale of *Rhododendron ponticum*

In spite of its great beauty, the Pontic Rhododendron needs
occasionally the curb of a strong hand.

WILLIAM BEAN, *Trees and Shrubs Hardy in the British Isles* (1916)

In June 2014 mountain rescue services in County Tipperary, southern Ireland, received a distress call. The two callers had earlier climbed the Knockmealdown Mountains and then chosen to shortcut eastwards towards the beautiful Bay Lough. The map showed no cliffs or impassable obstacles. Yet as they began descending towards the lough, they started encountering plants of *Rhododendron ponticum*. Just one or two at first, then a steadily thickening mass. Soon the plants were over their heads and they were fighting, sliding, dodging and tumbling their way past low branches as the slope got steeper. Too tired to attempt to climb back up, they had no option but to press on, until eventually they stopped, exhausted, and called for help. They had walked into a trap.

That particular thicket of *R. ponticum* is at least 350 metres (1,150 ft) in diameter, and is visible on Google Earth (and hence from space).[1] When the rescue team led by Ray Bradfield arrived at Bay Lough, the only way they could find the trapped hikers was to tell them, by phone, to vigorously shake the rhododendrons around them. The wobbling plants were spotted, right in the middle of the thicket. The rescuers had to hack their way towards them, progressing about 100 metres (330 ft) per half hour, periodically stopping to shake the plants so that watchers could locate and direct them. Finally they reached the hikers, and helped them move downwards, towards the lough side, which was by far the nearest exit. From here they were collected by the Cahir River Rescue team, and taken by boat to safety.[2]

Rhododendron ponticum stands alone among rhododendrons in its ability to spew forth its invading armies across the countryside. In Britain, *R. groenlandicum* has long been naturalized on bogs in Stirlingshire, and the yellow azalea *R. luteum* occasionally escapes in small numbers, but its inclusion in the list of invasive species whose planting is banned seems a gross overreaction.[3]

In contrast, *R. ponticum* forms huge naturalized populations in many parts of Britain and Ireland; it has also escaped cultivation in France, Belgium, Norway and New Zealand, though nowhere near on the same scale.[4] It can naturalize anywhere with acidic soils, but does best where there is high rainfall, hence its fondness for the British Isles in general, and the west side in particular. Large populations exist in Killarney and elsewhere in western Ireland, Snowdonia

Completion of the rescue of two hikers trapped in a thicket of *Rhododendron ponticum*, by Ireland's South Eastern Mountain Rescue Association.

Rhododendron luteum is a very rare garden escape in Britain, and even where it does escape, it is usually in the company of far greater numbers of R. *ponticum*, as at this site near Gairloch.

in Wales and parts of western Scotland.[5] If left alone, it eventually forms impenetrable thickets that shade out all other plants and are harmful to many animals, as well as the occasional hiker.[6] The seeds establish best where the soil is disturbed, and therefore they readily invade pine plantations, incurring great costs for the owner.[7]

Despite this impression of unchecked advancement, R. *ponticum* spreads relatively slowly, creating patchy populations close to a source of introduction. This is evident when driving through western Scotland, where one might not see a single plant for half an hour, then suddenly be driving through a mass of it. The spread, though slow, is inexorable. *New Scientist* magazine invited comparisons with John Wyndham's triffids, while conservation groups like The Conservation Volunteers (TCV) are always offering opportunities to spend a day or weekend 'rhoddy-bashing'.[8] War has been declared on R. *ponticum*. However, it is not quite as alien to Britain as many think.

Rhododendron ponticum occurs naturally in large numbers around the southeastern edge of the Black Sea, in northeast Turkey and Georgia. It becomes less common as one progresses westwards, always staying near the Black Sea, until one reaches outlying populations in Bulgaria. It also occurs in two small areas of Portugal, and one in southern Spain, plus a tiny patch in Lebanon.[9]

There is no doubt that all plants of R. *ponticum* found today in Britain and Ireland are descended from deliberate human introductions.[10] However, in the Irish fossil record lurks a surprise: R. *ponticum* was growing happily in some parts of southwestern Ireland around 400,000 years ago.[11] It is, therefore, far from a newcomer to the British Isles – merely a returning wanderer.

Some context is needed; go back far enough, and dinosaurs are native to Britain. Moreover, lions, hyenas, hippopotamuses, rhinos and elephants all roamed Britain around 125,000 years ago; all these were native more recently than *Rhododendron*![12] All of this results from dramatic natural climate swings over the past 2 million years, as our planet cycled from ice age to mild interglacial period and back again, driven by subtle metronomic fluctuations in its orbit termed Milankovich wobbles. During ice ages, sea levels dropped and Britain and Ireland were connected to mainland Europe, but the cold drove most species out, including R. *ponticum*. Many species retreated to the Mediterranean, much as some pensioners do during the British winter. Then as the

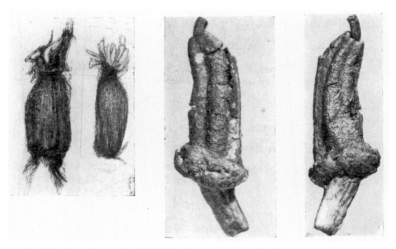

Fossil seeds and capsules of *Rhododendron ponticum* from before 350,000 years ago, preserved in an interglacial deposit near Gort, in western Ireland.

ice receded, they marched north again, but only species that moved quickly could reach Britain or Ireland before rising sea levels cut them off. When a particularly mild interglacial period began 374,000 years ago, R. ponticum was among those natural immigrants, but later the returning ice drove it out, and since then it has not repeated the feat. Perhaps its strategy of slow spreading let it down on these occasions. It thus shares with lions, hippos, elephants and dinosaurs the dubious status of being a former British Isles native.

Was southwestern Ireland, 400,000 years ago, also choked by a rhododendron monoculture, like the hill above Bay Lough today? There are reasons to think not. First, the fossil evidence suggests relatively few plants of R. ponticum peacefully coexisting with their neighbours.[13]

Second, clues may be found by looking at ericaceous plants whose range in Ireland today mirrors R. ponticum in the past. Three rare heather species occur only in and around Connemara in western Ireland, a bleak but beautiful, windswept landscape of jagged coastline, mountains and extensive bogs.[14] Erica erigena, the so-called Irish heath, has a few medium-sized populations in this area, and St Dabeoc's heath, Daboecia cantabrica, occurs on dry banks in and around Connemara. Even rarer is Erica mackaiana, which was first found by an exceptionally talented local botanist, William McAlla (or McCalla). McAlla was given by William Hooker the chance to join the ranks of great travelling plant hunters, but squandered it because of his terrible organizational skills.[15] Further south, in Killarney, the ericaceous strawberry tree Arbutus unedo is native in woodlands now threatened by invading R. ponticum.[16] Remarkably, all four species occur in the Mediterranean region, as R. ponticum still does, suggesting a broad similarity in climate range. The two Erica species might have been accidentally introduced by medieval smugglers, but none have spread like modern R. ponticum.[17]

So, R. ponticum did not spread rampantly when it was native, and nor do its ecologically comparable relatives. What, then, is different about the modern plant that makes it so ebulliently troublesome?

Artificially introduced plants often have an advantage over those that arrived naturally: they tend not to bring their natural predators or pathogens with them, while animals in their new range may not initially eat them. However, nothing much eats R. *ponticum* in its native range, and although several pathogens do attack it in Britain, none seem to check its spread.[18] Therefore, an explanation for its invasive behaviour must be sought elsewhere, and the one great difference between past interglacial periods and now is the presence of human beings. To what extent have we created this monster ourselves?

Having failed to do so naturally, R. *ponticum* returned to our shores on a boat from Spain in 1763, brought by the enterprising Dutchman Conrad Loddiges.[19] Other introductions followed, but DNA evidence confirms Spain and Portugal as the source of all *ponticum* plants growing wild in Britain.[20] It was brought to Ireland in or before 1800.[21]

In its early decades, R. *ponticum* was supposedly grown as a pot plant, valued for the ease with which it could be forced into early flowering, making it a useful and portable decoration for houses.[22] Meanwhile, plants of it were gradually gaining in size in the gardens of various nurserymen, who would later start crossing it with other species. The first known reports of self-sown R. *ponticum* are from 1841, from Dropmore in Buckinghamshire, in such numbers that it was 'very easy to fill woods with them', a claim that later events would conclusively support.[23] However, unidentified self-sown rhododendrons mentioned in 1829 may also have been R. *ponticum*.[24] Such rampant reproduction caused prices to plummet: the cost per plant in modern money was about £25 in 1800, but fell below £3 in the 1820s, and by 1850 was consistently well under £1.[25] Hence while the wealthy coveted the Sikkim Himalayan species, newly discovered by Hooker, and their cultivar offspring, the less well-off could also afford a rhododendron of their own . . . as long as it was *ponticum*.

In the latter half of the nineteenth century, R. *ponticum* began to appear outside of gardens, not as escapes but as deliberate plantings. One probable reason was the invention in 1861 of easy-to-load shotguns, which caused shooting as a pastime to take off rapidly.[26] Soon afterwards, abolition of duty on imported wood made home-grown timber less profitable, encouraging more woodlands to be adapted for shooting, which meant providing an evergreen shrub layer for game cover.[27] Hence vast numbers of evergreen shrubs were needed, and the cheaper the better. At first, *Mahonia aquifolium*, *Prunus*

Botanical painting of a naturalized *Rhododendron ponticum* by Janet Dyer, with hairs on the ovary providing clear evidence of the influence of at least one other species, most likely *R. catawbiense*.

laurocerasus and *Prunus lusitanica* were cheaper than R. *ponticum*,[28] but the plunging prices noted above were starting to change this. Evidently by 1864 some estates had ample rhododendrons, for one gun-toting lord is claimed to have killed 1,367 pheasants, 500 hares and some rabbits (apparently deemed unworthy of enumeration) in *a single day*, amid 'covers abounding in rhododendrons'.[29]

In the winter of 1880–81, the British weather took a hand. Portuguese laurels (*Prunus lusitanica*) took a battering during two severe cold snaps, killing off much of the above-ground growth, yet R. *ponticum* stands emerged largely unscathed.[30] It was now cheap and fast growing, avoided by hungry rabbits, produced attractive flowers and tolerated heavy shade. Suddenly nothing but R. *ponticum* would do for game cover, and everyone wanted to get hold of it. Those lucky enough to have adult plants of it growing on their estates turned a tidy profit selling on seedlings, making the price drop even further, down to 20 shillings per thousand (7 pence each in modern money).[31] This in turn allowed their use to be expanded, for example to lining driveways and decorating pleasure grounds, and as hardy grafting stock for more delicate species and cultivars.[32] The Surrey-based painter George Marks depicted it in at least two of his paintings. For a decade or two, R. *ponticum* was absolutely the plant to have.

Popularity, as ever, brought discord. People began to grumble that R. *ponticum* might perhaps be just a little *too* good at spreading and multiplying. On estates it was overrunning areas reserved for more delicate plants, while one writer complained of 'such a tangled mass of branches that it is anything but pleasant quarters for game', and that it made the game harder to flush out.[33]

Now the weather intervened once again, as Britain experienced one of the coldest winters of the century, in 1894–5. February shivered at an average temperature of $-1.8°C$, the second coldest February on record and the coldest monthly average since 1814.[34] Ice floes blocked the Thames, deep water pipes froze solid and death rates jumped among children and the elderly, not to mention bulbs at Kew.[35] This time, large numbers of R. *ponticum* plants were killed or maimed by

An invasion begins: young plants of *Rhododendron ponticum* by Loch Linnhe, western Scotland.

frost, leaving them 'an ugly brown, and dead to the ground' according to one furious writer, who also called them 'frauds' for their claimed hardiness.[36] From this point on, its popularity began to wane, but by then its grip on the British countryside had been firmly established.

As the twentieth century dawned, the spread of R. *ponticum* continued apace, only now increasingly under its own steam. Plantings throughout the countryside were layering outwards and producing armies of seedlings. By 1910 one plant had spread to a 24-metre (80-ft) diameter by layering.[37] In 1912 R. *ponticum* was 'quite at home' in the native woodlands of Killarney, and in 1916 Bean knew of places 'overrun with the shrub to such an extent as to have become monotonous'.[38] In 1924 the director of Forestry for Wales called it the worst weed in the country.[39]

Deliberate planting in the countryside had more or less ceased by this point, but some populations may have originated as late as the Second World War, when large rhododendrons were unceremoniously evicted from gardens to make way for 'Digging for Victory'. Dumped in the wild, some of these took root.[40]

Some populations sprung up where it had not even been knowingly planted, because of its popularity as grafting stock for more delicate species. Often the delicate species would be killed by frost, or simply overwhelmed by its more vigorous symbiont, converting whole plantings of choice hybrids into 'an area of about ten acres of R. *ponticum* where a bulldozer would be necessary to clear a path'.[41] A similar thing even happened in California, to the abject horror of Halfdan Lem, who had supplied the plants.[42] The phrase 'reverting to type like a *ponticum* rhododendron', describing something trying and failing to be what it wasn't, was later used in parliament by both Lord Soames (1985) and his MP son Nicholas (2000), and then again on TV by the latter in 2016, referring to Boris Johnson.[43] However, R. *ponticum* was still being recommended by some as the best possible grafting stock as late as 1933.[44]

By the 1930s the Forestry Commission, followed by Scottish landowners in 1950 and conservationists in the 1960s, were trying to control the plant.[45] Even rhododendrophiles like the Cowan family admitted that it was 'emphatically one of the most troublesome weeds'.[46] The plant historian Maggie Campbell-Culver in 2001 summed it up:

> it gradually revealed its true character – that of a killer, a smotherer, a choker-to-death of native woodland species and no plant for polite society. In its search for new victims it also spread along railway embankments, where its only merit is that one can sometimes see the wide variation of colour, from wishy-washy mauve to wishy-washy pink.[47]

The *Sunday Sport* tabloid, however, was possibly exaggerating when it contrived an article calling the 'ponticum strain' a 'deadly danger' to the Queen Mother.[48] The lady herself, who knew quite a bit about rhododendrons, would probably have been amused.[49]

Rhododendron ponticum, therefore, had significant help in establishing itself in the British countryside, but that cannot account for the

KILLER PLANTS STALK QUEEN MUM

CHELSEA FLOWER SHOW SHOCKER

Freak of nature puts royal in deadly danger

THE Queen Mum has been put at risk by a deadly plague of mutant shrubs.

A Triffid-like strain of the humble rhododendron is taking over her favourite gardens in killer clumps up to 20ft high.

And just one royal sniff of the scented shrub could send the 87-year-old great-grandma tumbling into her herbacious borders.

Armies of the shrubs, caused by a freak of nature, are towering above her favourite plot at Windsor Castle.

By JACK CANT

The deceptively beautiful purple bloom of the Ponticum strain has found its evil way into the gardens the Queen Mum planned and built with her late husband King George VI.

"They spread like wildlife, like something out of a horror movie," said Forestry Commission spokesman Steve O'Neill.

Deadly

"They kill anything that comes in their path," said the boffin, who does not know about the danger to the Queen Mum.

DANGER . . . Queen Mum

The problem has also struck at Exmoor National Park, where emergency teams of workmen have been sent to tackle the deadly shrub.

"It's been getting worse and it's not just in national parks, it's also found in Stately home gardens," said conservation manager Jeff Haynes.

"It is poisonous to mammals, birds and insects, and when it takes hold, everything else dies.

"We are extremely concerned — the plant has run riot."

The green-fingered royal has yet to be warned about the killer plant which has ravaged an area the size of Coventry in the last year.

Warned

"Yes, we've seen the Ponticum at Windsor. But we had no idea it was so dangerous," said a concerned royal workman.

The Queen Mum is expected to make her annual visit to the Chelsea Flower show tomorrow.

But one of the show's organisers warned: "There will be masses of rhododendrons at the exhibition."

A somewhat sensational article from UK tabloid the *Sunday Sport.*

rampant ease with which it subsequently spread, especially given that this seems not to have happened in Ireland 400,000 years ago. A clue comes from Turkey, where it has started to behave invasively *despite* being native, in woods where timber is extracted.[50] The only possible explanation is that alteration to the habitat and landscape, by human activity, benefits *R. ponticum*. The same thing is happening with *R. maximum* in the Appalachians.[51] Likewise native British species, such as ragwort, bracken and gorse, can become invasive under certain land management regimes. Human activity throws things out of balance, favouring some species and inhibiting others. Grazing animals quickly learn not to eat *R. ponticum*, whereas overgrazing, as by sika deer in Killarney and sheep elsewhere, churns up the soil, creating seedling establishment sites, which help it to invade.[52] *R. ponticum* is far better suited to the British Isles now than it was 400,000 years ago.

Humans may have inadvertently helped *R. ponticum* in another way: genetic modification. Look carefully at naturalized populations, at least in northern Britain, and you will come across the occasional hairy ovary, or dark crimson flecks on petals – characters absent in native Spanish populations. These show a genetic influence from other species, such as *R. catawbiense*, *R. maximum* and *R. arboreum*. This influence is greatest in Scotland, and almost absent in Ireland. Based on a genetic marker, the average British *ponticum* plant might contain about 5 per cent DNA from *R. catawbiense*, meaning that perhaps one or two of its great-great-great-grandparents were *R. catawbiense*.[53] Some individuals may have an ancestor that is *maximum* or *arboreum*, too.

This is a consequence of both deliberate and accidental hybridization in gardens during the nineteenth century. As noted in earlier chapters, *R. ponticum* was regularly used in cultivar creation, but also would have crossed naturally with any related species growing beside it, especially if only one individual was present. Among the masses of Victorian self-sown '*ponticum*' seedlings reported above would have been natural hybrids with *catawbiense*, and backcrosses from these to *R. ponticum*. These in turn would breed with other *ponticum* individuals nearby, spreading and diluting the genetic influence of *R. catawbiense*.

Natural selection may also have played a part. The hard winter of 1895 seems to have killed pure *ponticum* plants, while leaving hardy hybrids such as 'Cunningham's White' (*catawbiense* x *ponticum*) intact.[54] It had been known for a while that *R. catawbiense* and its hybrids were more frost tolerant than *R. ponticum*, and this has since been proved empirically.[55] When the savage winter of 1895 hit, natural selection favoured those individuals with frost-tolerance genes from *R. catawbiense*, just as it did 'Cunningham's White', over pure *ponticum*. After 1895 the surviving *ponticum* populations would then have comprised the more frost-hardy survivors, which might explain why no one reported similar damage to *ponticum* individuals following the equally severe winter of 1963.[56] The strength of selection probably varied with local climate, being strongest in chilly eastern Scotland, and weakest in the mild west of Ireland, leading to a greater influence from *catawbiense* in colder parts. Hence hybridization may have helped *R. ponticum* to expand northwards, and up the mountainsides.

Because British *ponticum* plants vary from completely pure *ponticum* to those containing perhaps 20 per cent DNA of another species, it is incorrect to call them '*Rhododendron* x *superponticum*'.[57] The coining of this name has caused regrettable confusion, wrongly implying that

A naturalized plant of *Rhododendron ponticum* near Gairloch, northwest Scotland, with very dark red corolla flecks. This character is not seen in pure native populations, and therefore indicates a genetic influence from other species.

all British *ponticum* plants are recent hybrids.[58] The correct way to describe them is R. *ponticum* with varying genetic influences from R. *catawbiense* and other species.

Rhododendron ponticum expunges other plants from the vicinity by the simple dint of shading them out. Adult trees may escape this effect, but in places like Killarney, forests could still be replaced by pure *ponticum* stands eventually, because a thick enough *ponticum* understorey stops regeneration of other species, including trees.[59] It impacts bird diversity and draws pollinators away from native plants, also inhibiting earthworms and soil microorganisms.[60] There is some evidence for allelopathy – the secretion of chemicals into the soil to suppress other plants – but it is far from clear whether this has any effect in the wild.[61] More likely is that R. *ponticum* drains the soil of nutrients, aided by its efficient fungal partners, making it difficult for other seeds to establish even after the *ponticum* has been removed. This

Rhododendron maximum, a species that probably contributed genes to Britain's invasive R. *ponticum* populations. From an 1806 edition of *Curtis's Botanical Magazine*.

A thriving infestation of *Rhododendron ponticum* near the royal residence at Sandringham, Norfolk.

is why eradication programmes tend to have to follow extermination of adult plants with successive sweeps to remove *Rhododendron* seedlings, until the soil recovers and natural vegetation can re-establish.

Ecologists are right to be concerned, for *R. ponticum* invades globally or nationally rare habitats, such as quaking bogs and transition meres, dry English heathlands and Atlantic rainforests in western Scotland that are home to rare mosses and lichens.[62] The endemic Lundy cabbage (*Coincya wrightii*), which grows only on Lundy Island, is losing ground to invading *R. ponticum*.[63]

It also wreaks economic havoc. In Argyll and Bute, 3,300 hectares (8,150 acres) of commercial woodland (mainly pine plantations) are infested with *ponticum*, adding greatly to the cost of timber extraction.[64] In large park gardens, especially those that showcase less aggressive rhododendrons (that is, any that are not *ponticum*), often money has to be spent cutting back *ponticum* to stop it taking over, as at Isabella Plantation and Windsor Great Park.[65] Likewise, outside of gardens it has to be hacked back to preserve footpaths and walking routes. Sheep can suffer fatal poisoning if they eat it, though where

A breathtaking display of colour from naturalized *Rhododendron ponticum* at Bay Lough, Ireland. It was here that the hikers became trapped in June 2014.

it is common they learn to avoid it, and, as noted previously, they can be cured by a good cup of tea.

Recently a new problem has emerged: a disease called sudden oak death, caused by *Phytophthora ramorum* and its relative *P. kernoviae*.[66] These fungus-like pathogens attack a wide range of woody species including beech, oak and larch. *Rhododendron ponticum* is the 'Typhoid Mary' of this disease, easily infected but barely harmed, acting as a reservoir of infection for other species nearby, including other more delicate rhododendrons.[67]

Fighting back, however, is neither easy nor cheap. Manual removal of plants is possible, and in this way a voluntary group called Groundwork removed 40 per cent of *ponticum* cover from Killarney since 1981, before they were stymied by bureaucracy.[68] Removing the largest populations may require industrial-scale methods: mechanical diggers, fire and herbicides. The cost of eradication from Snowdonia alone was estimated at £30 to 45 million.[69] Waiting to act also has a price; the estimated £9.3 million cost of eradicating it now from Argyll and Bute would double by 2028, and treble again by 2058, because of the relentless growth and spread of the plant.[70] Partial control costs less, but is only a holding action. Given the costs, eradication is most feasible and worthwhile where a discrete population threatens an important nature site, as at Sunart in Scotland.[71] Possibly, the spread of the plant could also be checked by the simple expedient of reducing grazing pressure, be it from sheep or deer, and otherwise minimizing the disturbance that helps its seedlings to establish.

Not everyone sees *R. ponticum* as a monster requiring summary extermination. In a poll of public opinion about whether control should be applied to fifteen damaging and non-native plant and animal species in Scotland, *R. ponticum* was one of only three for which opinions about control were clearly divided, with only 51 per cent supporting control measures, and just 12 per cent strongly supporting them.[72] The other two were birds: Canada goose and ruddy duck. Support for control was higher for supposedly cuddly species like the grey squirrel, American mink or introduced hedgehogs on Orkney, and highest of all for two other plants, Japanese knotweed and giant hogweed. Hence in the public perception of invasive plants, *R. ponticum* is an anomaly: a lot of people seem to like it.

The hiker-trapping population around Bay Lough in Ireland illustrates the stunning beauty of a large *ponticum* population in full bloom, showing why local people might like to keep them around. Removal of large populations of *ponticum* from around Loch Torridon in northwest Scotland upset many local residents, while ecologists and park managers took several years to persuade local people to support control measures in Snowdonia.[73] Even a few animal species do sometimes benefit from its presence, including nightingales, otters and badgers.[74]

At Whitley Park near Huddersfield, local people mounted a spirited defence of three copses of *R. ponticum*, albeit as part of a larger saga involving alleged destruction of native vegetation by the park's owners, and possible badger setts under the copse. A letter to a local newspaper described as 'spectacular' the floral display from these rhododendron copses.[75] In parliament, local MP David Hinchliffe described how this saga ended:

> The local residents attempted to stand in front of the bull-dozers and to open their doors, but it was to no avail – within three hours, three circular copses, well-loved features of the Whitley park estate for at least 100 years, had been destroyed.[76]

Supported by neighbouring MP Barry Sheerman and minister Angela Eagle, Mr Hinchliffe concluded:

> I recognise that, despite their attractiveness, especially at this time of year, rhododendrons are regarded by some as an invasive weed. I understand the need to exercise control, particularly if their growth suppresses natural tree regeneration, but such control should be exercised by ongoing and sensitive removal of the vegetation concerned, not by what the local parish council chairman described as 'environmental vandalism'.[77]

Rhododendron ponticum, therefore, divides opinion like few other plants in Britain. It provides a beautiful spectacle, which few wild British plants – native or otherwise – can match. It creates natural playgrounds for children. Yet the detrimental effects on wildlife and forestry are unarguable, and left unchecked it will continue its relentless spread.

There is little point spending millions on removing the plant only to leave a wasteland behind. Rhododendrons hold the soil firmly in place and trap rainwater like a natural forest, so removing them will increase rainwater run-off.[78] By contrast, a hillside perpetually overgrazed by sheep supports barely more biological diversity, but is far more prone to erosion and allows rapid run-off of rainwater, contributing to the flooding problems that have plagued Britain over recent years.[79] Rhododendron wood has potential as a biofuel, whereas possibly £850 per hectare (£344 per acre) per year could be earned by harvesting *ponticum* populations for the foliage trade.[80]

Decisions about controlling *R. ponticum* need to be made with intelligence. Populations in parks, like Whitley Park or Richmond Park, give more than they take, and some Scottish populations exist in a landscape that has little value beyond scenery, which *ponticum* enhances. Control should be deployed where there is a specific local need. In light of this, proposed EU legislation banning the sale or planting of this species anywhere within the EU would not be especially helpful, given that the species is native in Spain, Portugal and Bulgaria, where it is also endangered. A further suggestion to include its hybrids in the ban, probably inspired by the erroneous name of *R.* x *superponticum*, would be disastrous for horticulture, banning, for example, the innocent 'Cunningham's White' cultivar which has replaced pure *ponticum* as preferred grafting stock, and has never once been seen growing wild anywhere in Britain.[81]

A curious coda to the tale of *R. ponticum* was provided by the Turner Prize-winning artist Simon Starling in the year 2000. He carefully dug up seven plants from a naturalized population on Elrick Hill in Scotland that was scheduled for destruction, and drove them all the way to one of the native Spanish sites.[82] The title of this artistic work reads like that of a scientific paper, perhaps intentionally:

Rescued Rhododendrons (7 *Rhododendron ponticum* plants rescued from Elrick Hill, Scotland and transported to Parque Los Alcornocales, Spain, from where they were introduced into cultivation in 1763 by Claes Alstroemer).

As conceptual art it succeeds in asking questions; in particular, whether introducing Scottish plants that might contain genes from *R. catawbiense* into pure native populations is a good idea. Conservation purists would say no, but pragmatists might counter that it could help the fragile native populations react to climate change, which poses a severe threat (see next chapter). Given how much better they grow in Scotland than Spain, the 'rescued' plants might not have appreciated Starling's efforts. An Irish art student named Roisin Byrne would later dig up one of Starling's plants and fly it to Ireland, as part of a study challenging modern art through deliberate theft and plagiarism.[83]

nine
Conservation, Collections and the Future

> It was found that the suitable bioclimatic envelope for Rhododendron has shrunk considerably under the envisaged climate change scenario.[1]

I n the late 1920s, a train pulled in at Scotland's most remote railway station, Corrour, and from it were unloaded thousands of rhododendron seedlings. These would have begun their lives in China, as seeds collected from wild plants by George Forrest's team.

Even now, their journey was not over. Most had a long wait there as, group by group, they were carried by horse and cart along a mile of track to Loch Ossian. There, at last, a steam boat would carry them to their final home on the steep southeastern shores of the loch. The architect of all this was Sir John Stirling Maxwell, baronet and owner of the estate. He had been among the sponsors of Forrest's sixth expedition, and would sponsor others in the coming years.[2] He would succeed in his goal to create a rhododendron garden on his lands, and perhaps he achieved something greater. For among those fragile saplings that survived the long journey were species that now face a very uncertain future in the wild, such as *R. insigne*. The little plants of this species shivering by the station at Corrour were refugees, escaping the forces that would destroy their parent populations.

Corrour is a private estate, but a visitor approaching it along the southern side of the lake would first witness normal Scottish country-side: towering hillside slopes clad in grass, rushes and mosses, a vast

Diverse *Rhododendron* species thriving on a remote hillside above Loch Ossian in the Corrour estate.

body of cool clear water, plus the inevitable pine plantations and, in summer, midges. Then, rhododendron plants would start to appear, which the discerning observer would quickly realize were not *R. ponticum*. Soon the walker would be standing among an astonishing array of rhododendron diversity, eclipsing even the hill slopes of northwest Yunnan. In this one, seemingly wild place grow 125 species of *Rhododendron*. Indeed, to walk among these is to come as close as one can to experiencing the thrill of walking through Himalayan forests, without actually leaving Britain. Though technically a garden, this place feels truly wild.

Successive owners after Sir John loved the rhododendrons, but only the most recent has been proactive in ensuring their welfare. Drainage needs to be carefully maintained, otherwise great specimens like the now huge *R. insigne* plant could succumb to waterlogging in this foreign land. Where species have been lost, new ones are being planted by the Rhododendron Species Conservation Group.[3]

Corrour is the most dramatic of many private collections of rhododendrons in Britain and beyond. Others include Glendoick,

Inverewe and numerous gardens in Cornwall.[4] Together with botanic
gardens, these have a role to play in preserving the incredible diversity
of species that exist within *Rhododendron*.

To read of the excursions and adventures of plant collectors of the
past brings perhaps a longing for days that are gone. There is the thrill
of discovery, coupled with the witnessing of untamed landscapes,
brimming full of pristine nature. For example, from Kingdon-Ward:

> I sat down on the mountain slope beneath bushes of rhodo-
> dendron aflame with blossom; numbers of tits chirped and
> hopped from bush to bush, poking their heads inside the
> blotched flowers, seeking small beetles. When the dazzle of
> sunset had been replaced by violet dusk, I looked westwards
> across the Mekong valley to the sacred mountain of Ka Karpo,
> and saw cataracts of splintered ice frozen to the cliffs over
> which they plunged; close to the foot of the biggest glacier
> were several houses scattered over terraces of shining corn.[5]

Increasingly, such passages provide stark and unwelcome contrast
with today's world. Then, the natural world seemed to grow and
expand with every expedition, such as Kingdon-Ward's connection
of the Tsangpo and Brahmaputra rivers, and there was always the
feeling that more awaited discovery, as illustrated by Forrest's ongoing
search for the 'home' of the Rhododendrons. Now, wild places are
in retreat, disappearing beneath an ever-expanding human population, some hungry for food, others merely for profit. Forests are
felled, marshes are drained, and grasslands 'improved'. There may yet
be a few new rhododendrons to discover, but if not found soon these
might disappear, forever unremarked and unloved.

Parts of China were already undergoing very rapid deforestation
by 1945, and a poor policy decision in Nepal in 1957 has led to rapid
(about 2 per cent per year) deforestation ever since.[6] Even harvesting
practices that have been sustainable for countless generations, such

as the gathering of rhododendrons for firewood and incense in the Sikkim Himalaya, are starting to damage wild populations because of constantly expanding human populations.[7] Happily, some places like the Tsangpo Gorges, where Kingdon-Ward found so many exciting species, appear to be largely intact, that same inaccessibility that made them so exciting now helping to protect them.[8] However, proposed hydroelectric projects present a threat, and it must be hoped that they move forward with sensitivity.[9]

China is taking steps to protect its wild heritage. A massive habitat restoration programme in the Loess Plateau, for example, is benefiting wildlife, local people and the global climate.[10] The cultural importance of rhododendrons adds extra impetus to their preservation. The Baili Azalea scenic area of Guizhou province, China, sits on top of coal seams, and but for its rhododendrons, it would probably now be an open-cast mine. Instead, it receives countless tourists every spring to see the flowering of the *delavayi* x *irroratum* hybrid population. The beauty of the plants has protected all of the nature around them, and even the way of life of the local farmers.

A garden of planted Rhododendron species, not native to the area, at Baili, China. The darker trees in the background are the locally native *R. delavayi*.

Boschniakia himalaica, a root parasite growing under its host plants *Rhododendron delavayi* and *R. irroratum* in Baili Azalea Nature Reserve, Guizhou, China.

In the Chinese tourist industry, however, there is not the clear distinction between wild places and gardens that one finds elsewhere. Visitors come to see the rhododendrons, and are not too fussed if they are planted or wild. Baili now has an azalea garden full of species like R. *molle* that are not native to the area, planted to enhance the experience for visitors. It is surrounded by natural rhododendron populations, making it highly likely that some of these immigrants will interbreed with the native species. The extremely rare R. *bailiense*, whose global population comprises two tiny patches in Baili,[11] could disappear as a pure species within a few generations, replaced by hybrids, if non-native relatives were planted nearby.

Rhododendrons are not merely valuable in the wild for their own sake. As dominant vegetation components, they support a community of other organisms. There is even a parasitic plant, *Boschniakia himalaica*, that grows exclusively on the roots of rhododendrons, and has sacrificed its leaves and chlorophyll in favour of this felonious lifestyle.[12] The catch is that it cannot survive without its host. In Turkey, a few sites exist where the much-maligned *Rhododendron ponticum* forms the climax species of natural rhododendron-dominated woodland, with specimens more than 500 years old, supporting one of the most rare and threatened vegetation communities in western Eurasia.[13]

The relationship between horticulture and conservation has not always been a happy one. Overcollecting for gardens has decimated some species, and various protected areas in China, including the Baili Azalea scenic area, are now being rapidly stripped of their orchid floras by locals who sell them to visitors.[14] Ernest Wilson responded to the sight of tens of thousands of regal lilies by taking the bulbs of 6,000 of them,[15] but that was an age when the natural world still seemed indestructible, and its resources inexhaustible.

Now, amid the awareness of threats to biodiversity, rules exist restricting collection in many places. While well intended, such rules often hinder those with noble goals, while the less scrupulous simply ignore them, like the orchid plunderers at Baili. In Vietnam, laws against collecting are so strict and inflexible that several rare endemic species such as R. *fansipanensis* and R. *suilenhense* have never been legally collected, and therefore cannot formally be described as species.[16] Hence they do not officially exist, cannot be included in red lists of endangered species, and are therefore denied some of the protection due to them.

Rhododendrons, unlike bulbs or orchids, can be collected without causing any harm to wild populations. The size of the plants, and the prolific way they set seed, ensured that there would be no stripping of whole plants from the countryside where they occurred. A collector like Hooker could gather tens of thousands of seeds from one individual plant, without really harming its reproductive effort for that year, let alone its lifetime. Hence a balance is needed, allowing collection by trusted persons, ideally with local participation, as has occurred in China since 1981. Otherwise, cultivated plants raised from technically illegal seed collections in Vietnam of R. *fansipanensis* might one day be the only ones left in existence, if its native habitat is destroyed. Likewise, some species may soon, if not already, survive only because of seed brought back by Wilson, Forrest and others.

Some *Rhododendron* species may already have vanished from the wild. Certainly extinct worldwide is R. *retrorsipilum*, a vireya whose small area of occurrence in Papua New Guinea has been completely deforested, and which sadly was not brought into cultivation before this happened. Also gone from the wild but happily surviving in cultivation is R. *kanehirae*, which once adorned sunny rocks along the Peishi River in northern Taiwan. A further 36 more taxa (species, subspecies or varieties) are now formally listed as 'Critically Endangered' while 280 are 'Vulnerable' or 'Endangered'. The 'Critically Endangered' category includes those that have not been seen for a while in the wild, and which may already be extinct there due to habitat loss. These include R. *auritum*, R. *searsiae*, the aforementioned R. *insigne* var. *insigne*, R. *eurysiphon*, R. *shweliense* and R. *griersonianum* (parent to many fine hybrids), all of them from China.[17]

Critically endangered rhododendrons that are preserved in cultivation: *R. auritum*, *R. searsiae* and *R. insigne* var. *insigne*.

Were the genus of lesser horticultural significance, most or all of these species might be gone forever. Instead, they have bought themselves a stay of execution through their beauty, and the efforts of those who were captivated by them. Some of these may yet hang on in undiscovered populations somewhere, but if not then their future rests entirely in the various gardens, both public and private, scientific and personal, where living specimens exist. This is termed *ex situ* conservation: preserving a species outside its natural range and habitat.

Leading this effort is the Royal Botanic Garden, Edinburgh, with well over 500 species.[18] Besides the original Edinburgh garden with its moderately cool climate, this organization also runs the rugged hillside garden in the Borders at Dawyck, the steep highland garden of Benmore, and the extraordinary garden of Logan in the extreme southwest of Scotland, where the oceanic climate allows palm trees to thrive – a most unexpected sight in Scotland. Here, tender species that need glasshouses elsewhere can grow outdoors, like the rhododendron Maddenia group and the rare *R. petrocharis*. Meanwhile, private gardens like Inverewe, Corrour and Glendoick between them have species collections to rival Edinburgh, while both Kew and the Sir Harold Hillier Gardens are especially well represented for *Pentanthera* azaleas.

Whether in a species' natural range or beyond it, conservation requires more than just keeping one or two individuals alive; genetic diversity is essential. Without it, the species cannot respond through natural selection to threats like disease or climate change. Conservation, therefore, must preserve a whole population. For many rhododendrons, the scattering of individuals across so many collections, both private and public, is of major importance. Even better are new seed collections from wild populations, greatly increasing genetic diversity in cultivation. Kunming Institute of Botany are doing this in China, and it is starting to happen in India with species like *R. maddenii*.[19]

If cultivated plants are to play any role in conservation of a species, accurate labelling is essential, otherwise they become just an attractive but enigmatic shrub. The Valley Gardens at Windsor Great Park owe their conservation value to the meticulous labelling of J. B. Stevenson, who during the early twentieth century had assembled a remarkable collection of *Rhododendron* species at Tower Hill.[20] When Eric Savill was commissioned to create The Valley Gardens by King George VI and Queen Elizabeth, he bought J. B.'s collection from his widow, Roza. Many of the plants had attained full size by then, and transporting the largest specimen, a 1.5 ton (3,310 lb) *R. falconeri*, to Windsor was a huge undertaking, reminiscent of a *Thunderbirds* episode. Only

Rhododendron petrocharis, a tender species considered vulnerable in the wild, growing outdoors at Logan near Stranraer in southwest Scotland. Logan is a satellite garden of the Royal Botanic Gardens, Edinburgh.

13 km (8 miles) as the crow flies, the journey was several times longer as low bridges had to be avoided, and telegraph wires often needed to be lifted to let the plant pass.[21] It was worth the effort, for the setting – a series of little ridges and valleys overlooking Virginia Water – is stunning.

A special mention must go to Glendoick, between Dundee and Perth in Scotland. Almost uniquely, it keeps alive several of the traditions described in this book: the commercial collector, the collecting travelogue books and the family business. Euan Cox collected with Farrer in Burma (Myanmar),[22] and his son Peter was part of the first full collecting expedition to China after it began opening up again, in 1981. Now Peter's son Kenneth runs the nursery with his wife, and in 1998 Kenneth retraced Kingdon-Ward's epic journey through the Tsangpo Gorges, refinding many original rhododendron locations.[23] Glendoick has a magnificently diverse collection of *Rhododendron* species, and has supplied several to Corrour to further boost the species diversity there.

Cultivars may be a human construct, but then so is the Sphinx, and the Mona Lisa. Rhododendron cultivars are works of art that many

Members of the Rhododendron Species Conservation Group planting various species at Corrour. All the young plants seen on the path were supplied by Glendoich.

Some of the Azalea cultivars in the Kew Collection.

are keen to preserve, especially the earliest ones, providing as they do connections to pioneer breeders like the Waterers and Veitches. Because named hybrid cultivars are a single clone, they cannot be reproduced by seed; keeping them going requires dedicated effort via cuttings. Many cultivars have been lost forever, with vireyas probably the hardest hit due to their need for glasshouse space. To recreate them from scratch would be akin to forging a Van Gogh. Hence the efforts, for example, of Archie Skinner to preserve as many old Ghent azalea and Rustica cultivars as possible, at Sheffield Park in Sussex.[24]

Not everyone agreed. Kingdon-Ward felt that hybrids of all kinds paled beside species,[25] while Waterer Nursery manager G. H. Pinckney in 1953 asserted that:

View towards the sea at Trebah, Cornwall, with huge specimens of *Rhododendron arboreum* and its hybrids in flower.

If all growers were more particular in eliminating those varieties superseded as no longer worthy of garden merit as soon as possible, the public would be better off in being able to select their plants from a smaller and choicer list than now meets the bewildered amateur eye.[26]

All of the gardens mentioned above preserve many cultivars. Cornish gardens conserve and display tender but lovely cultivars; for example, Trebah has 'Fragrantissimum', 'Lady Alice Fitzwilliam', 'Glory of Penjerrick' and many others in a spectacular setting. Penjerrick itself is close by, full of rhododendrons, and open to the public. However, after the National Trust declined to purchase it, the owners have allowed it to become semi-wild. It is a place of great character, but knowledge of precisely what it contains could disappear.

In Baili, China, local legend has it that one year there came a great flood, and afterwards no one could find fuel. Moved by the desperate plight of their neighbours, one kindly couple walked into a cave and transformed themselves into coal, which warmed their communities ever after. A sky fairy was so moved by their sacrifice that she spread holy rhododendron flowers in their honour.[27]

We now know, of course, that fossil fuels are both a blessing and a curse. Every ecosystem on Earth faces an existential threat from anthropogenic climate change, and a Chinese saying that the luck and prosperity of the Chengdu Plain will last until the snow disappears from the 6,710 metres (22,000 ft) holy mountain of Hsueh-po-ting is not as reassuring as it once was.[28] Climate change has already caused a substantial shift in flowering time for *R. arboreum* in India and Nepal, which could disrupt their interactions with animal pollinators, and hence the whole ecosystem.[29] The area of land in the Sikkim Himalaya that is suitable for rhododendron growth is predicted to shrink dramatically as the climate warms.[30]

The diversity of rhododendrons around Yunnan and the Himalayas was created by a diversity of microclimates, and the dramatic subdivision of the region by high ridges and deep, dry valleys. Climate change will alter those microclimates, while the same barriers that helped make the species will prevent many from shifting their range in response. Those that occur on the sides of hills can move upwards, and all plant species do have a range of conditions they can tolerate, depending in part upon what they are competing with. However, here, as elsewhere, the habitats for many have already been fragmented by human activity, and many plants hang on in patches surrounded by farmland or towns. If these patches start to become too hot or dry, it will not be so easy for them to move. *Rhododendron bailiense* clings to the side of a small hill just below its summit, but the summit is covered by an old hut and an impromptu rubbish dump. As the climate warms, the species will

Rhododendron in the snow at Edinburgh Botanic Gardens.

surely vanish from this spot; if it is to survive in the wild, it might need to be sown in a similar but cooler spot nearby. The little nursery of Mr Huang, a local enthusiast who played a key role in its discovery, may become vital to its survival.

As climate change begins to bite, it will become more and more difficult to conserve things in the exact spot where they are, and conservationists will have to ask themselves whether deliberate introductions to new ranges, where the climate now suits an organism, is the only way to keep some species alive in the wild. Sometimes, of course, this happens largely by accident: *R. ponticum* thrives in Britain while many native populations in Spain or Portugal are at their ecological limit, and will likely struggle to survive even modest local climatic warming. *Rhododendron triflorum* is flourishing and self-seeding at Corrour. The more the climate changes, the more likely it becomes that further species will grow better in their introduced range than in the native one.

Both examples raise a bigger question. *R. ponticum* is already genetically altered, and if left to their own devices the plants at Corrour will produce mainly hybrids. Yet the great breeding experiments of the last 200 years showed how hybridization can rapidly adapt plants to new surroundings, in very few generations. Natural selection, likewise, works much faster on hybrids because there is so much more diversity available from which beneficial gene combinations may emerge. This may be the only way for long-lived plants like rhododendrons to keep pace with rapid climate change. From natural hybrid zones like that at Baili, and artificial species gatherings like that at Corrour, may come new evolutionary lines of mixed ancestry, adapting to a warming and unstable world. Nurserymen have spent two centuries trying to breed cold-tolerance into their rhododendron cultivars, but breeders of today might do well to turn their attentions to raising a new generation of rhododendrons able to withstand severe droughts and other extreme weather.

To an extent, we can defend both species and treasured cultivars in our gardens, through careful placement and loving care. Hence,

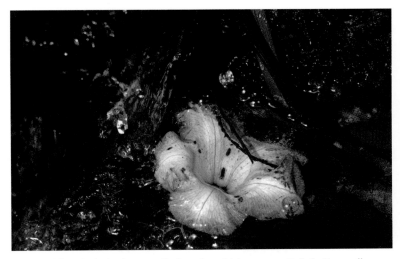

A fallen rhododendron corolla (set of petals) in water at Trebah, Cornwall.

spread across so many gardens on several continents, rhododendrons may seem well protected. However, it is as well to recall that during the two world wars, nations were stripped of their gardeners, and rhododendrons were turfed out of gardens to make way for food crops.[31] Anthony Waterer Junior turned the Knap Hill Nursery into a cattle farm during the First World War.[32] Climate change is already hitting global food production, both directly and indirectly (via political instability).[33] There is still time to bring it under control, otherwise the day will come when beauty in our gardens will once again be cast aside in favour of necessity, and this time perhaps forever. The future of rhododendrons, as with so much else, is in our hands.

Timeline

60 million years ago	First fossil evidence of *Rhododendron*
c. 5 million years ago	Rapid diversification of rhododendrons in and around Yunnan, western China, probably triggered by uplift of the Himalayas
400,000 years ago	*Rhododendron ponticum* grows naturally in western Ireland during an interglacial period
401 BC	Xenophon records the first known instance of mass poisoning by honey from rhododendrons (*ponticum* or *luteum*), involving the Greek army at Colchis
67 BC	Rhododendron honey used by Heptakometes, fighting for Mithradates, to incapacitate 1,000 Roman troops, who were then slaughtered
AD 1495	A Chinese text distinguishes twenty kinds of rhododendron
1656	*Rhododendron hirsutum* becomes the first species cultivated for ornament in Britain
1680	Botanical accounts describe the species now known as *Rhododendron indicum* and *R. viscosum*, from Japan (via cultivation in Holland) and North America respectively
1736	*Rhododendron maximum* is introduced to Britain from North America

1753	Linnaeus publishes *Species plantarum*, formally describing the first eleven *Rhododendron/Azalea* species, but making the fateful decision to make *Azalea* a genus separate from *Rhododendron*
1763	*Rhododendron ponticum* is introduced to Britain by Conrad Loddiges
1814	Nathaniel Wallich sends seeds of *Rhododendron arboreum* to Britain packed in sugar
1819	The first spontaneous rhododendron hybrid is recorded in cultivation, an 'Azaleodendron' cross, making clear the massive potential for rhododendron hybridization in cultivation
1824	The process of merging the genera *Rhododendron* and *Azalea* begins
1830s	Ghent azalea cultivar group, raised in Belgium, debuts in Britain
1843	Thomas Lobb begins importing tropical vireya rhododendrons to Britain, where Veitch Nurseries grows, hybridizes and commercializes them as glasshouse plants
1848–50	Joseph Hooker introduces 28 new *Rhododendron* species from the Himalayas
1869	Missionary botanist Père David arrives in Sichuan. His work, and that of Père Delavay who would follow, revealed to the West the floristic richness of China, including numerous new rhododendrons
1892	The cultivar 'Pink Pearl' is registered by Gomer Waterer. It will go on to become the most commercially successful rhododendron cultivar in history
1913	Veitch Nurseries closes down after more than 100 years
1918	Ernest Wilson introduces fifty Kurume azalea cultivars from Japan to Britain and North America

Timeline

1932	George Forrest dies in China at the end of his seventh expedition, having introduced more than 100 rhododendron species from China into cultivation
1938	*Rebecca* by Daphne du Maurier is published, with rhododendrons providing a sinister recurring theme
1950	Joseph Rock flees China following Mao's victory, bringing to an end the era of commercial collecting there
1981	Botanical expeditions resume in China, now with scientific intent, and involving Chinese botanists as leaders
1990	Phylogenetic studies begin recommending that the genera *Ledum* and *Menziesia* be included within *Rhododendron*
2010	Planting of *Rhododendron ponticum* in Britain is declared illegal because of its invasive character
2011	*Rhododendron retrorsipilum* from Papua New Guinea becomes the first *Rhododendron* species to be formally declared extinct
2015	Work on sequencing the complete genome of *Rhododendron ponticum* begins in Chengdu, China

Appendix: Table of Groups within *Rhododendron*

With more than 1,000 recognized species, some subdivision of *Rhododendron* has been necessary to help the scientist and the gardener to find their way around. This little summary table is provided in the hope that it will do the same for readers of this book. The table mostly follows the 1996 Edinburgh classification, except where clear scientific evidence has indicated that certain groups should be broken up, in which case this is followed. Only the first four major groups are horticulturally significant. In some cases, subgroups are indicated that have particular horticultural, scientific or cultural significance.

Major Group	Subgroup	Distribution	Approx no. of species	Example species
Subgenus *Rhododendron* ('Lepidotes')		Mostly China/Himalayas	465	*ferrugineum, hirsutum, cinnabarinum, rubiginosum, racemosum, yunnanense, maddenii, ciliatum, dauricum*
	Vireya group	Tropical Asia	313	*javanicum, jasminiflorum, malayanum, konori*
	Ledum group	Cold temperate	8	*tomentosum, groenlandicum*

Subgenus *Hymenanthes* ('Elepidotes')		Mostly China/ Himalayas	225	*arboreum, calophytum, fortunei, griffithianum.* Cultivars including 'Pink Pearl', Loderi group, 'Eleanor Cathcart'
	Subsection *Pontica*	NE Asia, Black Sea, N America	10	*ponticum, maximum, catawbiense, aureum, caucasicum, macrophyllum, degronianum,* 'Cunningham's White'
Subgenus *Tsutsusi*		Japan, China	81	*indicum, simsii, kiusianum, kaempferi,* Kurume azaleas
Subgenus *Pentanthera* (reduced)		Mostly N America (two in Eurasia)	16	*luteum, molle, periclymenoides, occidentale, arborescens, prinophyllum,* Ghent, Mollis, Knap Hill and Exbury azaleas
	Section *Rhodora*	Canada, Northern USA	1	*canadense (vaseyi* was placed here but may not belong)
Subgenus *Mumeazalea*		Japan	1	*semibarbatum* only
Subgenus *Candidastrum*		USA	1	*albiflorum* only

Subgenus *Therorhodion*		NE Asia, Alaska	I or 2	*camtschaticum* and the dubious *redowskianum*
Subgenus *Azaleastrum* (reduced)		Asia	5	*hongkongense, leptothrium, ngawchangense, ovatum, vialii*
Chionastrum group (previously in *Azaleastrum*)		Asia	11	*cavalieri, championae, esquirolii, feddei, hancockii, henryi, latoucheae, moulmainense, stamineum, tutcherae*
Former genus *Menziesia*		E Asia, N America	9	*multiflorum, pilosum, menziesii*
Uncertain Relationships (previously in *Pentanthera*)		Japan, Korea, N America, etc.	6	*albrechtii, schlippenbachii, quinquefolium, pentaphyllum, vaseyi, nipponicum*

References

Introduction: Beauty and Bane

1 Hui-Lin Li, *The Garden Flowers of China* (New York, 1959); Joseph Needham, *Science and Civilisation in China: Biology and Biological Technology, Part 1, Botany* (Cambridge, 1986), vol. VI, p. 438.

2 E. H. Schafer, 'Li Te-Yü and the Azalea', *Asiatische Studien*, XVIII–XIX (1965), pp. 105–14; Li, *The Garden Flowers of China*.

3 'Yang Chih Chu' in Chinese; Schafer, 'Li Te-Yü and the Azalea'; Li, *The Garden Flowers of China*.

4 Rose Blight, *Private Eye*, CDXXXI (23 June 1978), and CDXXIII (3 March 1978).

5 WriteLine LLC, 'Washington State Stamps', www.postcardsfrom.com, accessed 19 September 2015; and see 'Washington State Flower', www.50states.com, accessed 19 September 2015.

6 'West Virginia State Flower', www.50states.com, accessed 19 September 2015.

7 Feng Guomei, *Rhododendrons of China* (Beijing, 1988), vol. I, pp. 3–4.

1 Sex and the Single Rhododendron

1 Dr Maria Chamberlain, pers. comm.

2 Judith Taylor, *Visions of Loveliness: Great Flower Breeders of the Past* (Athens, OH, 2014), p. 128.

3 D. F. Chamberlain, 'A Revision of *Rhododendron*. II. Subgenus *Hymenanthes*', *Notes from the Royal Botanic Garden Edinburgh*, XXXIX (1982), pp. 265 and 328.

4 R. Cruden and K. Jensen, 'Viscin Threads, Pollination Efficiency and Low Pollen-ovule Ratios', *American Journal of Botany*, LXVI (1979), pp. 875–9.

5 J. Padrutt et al., 'Postpollination Reproductive Biology of *Rhododendron prinophyllum* (Small) Millais', *Journal of the American Society for Horticultural Science*, CXVII (1992), pp. 656–62.

6 *Kalmia* is more closely related to the heathers (*Erica* and *Calluna*) than it is to *Rhododendron*; K. A. Kron, 'Phylogenetic Relationships of

Rhododendroideae (Ericaceae)', *American Journal of Botany*, LXXXIV (1997), pp. 973–80.

7 M. L. Grant et al., 'Is there Such a Thing as *Kalmia* x *Rhododendron?*', *Journal of the American Society for Horticultural Science*, CXXIX (2004), pp. 517–22; M. L. Grant et al., '*Kalmia* x *Rhododendron* Debunked', RHS *Rhododendron, Camellia and Magnolia Yearbook* (2005), pp. 25–31.

8 Frederick Street, *Hardy Rhododendrons* (London, 1954), pp. 20 and 67.

9 R. I. Milne et al., 'A Hybrid Zone Dominated by Fertile F$_1$s: Maintenance of Species Barriers in *Rhododendron*', *Molecular Ecology*, XII (2003), pp. 2719–29; R. I. Milne and R. J. Abbott, 'Reproductive Isolation Among Two Interfertile *Rhododendron* Species: Low Frequency of Post-F$_1$ Hybrid Genotypes in Alpine Hybrid Zones', *Molecular Ecology*, XVII (2008), pp. 1108–21.

10 Street, *Hardy Rhododendrons*, p. 87.

11 Ibid., p. 19.

12 Sir Giles Loder, '*Rhododendron* Loderi and its Varieties and Hybrids', www.rhododendrons.com, 1950, accessed 24 January 2017.

13 J. G. Melton, *Faiths Across Time: 5,000 Years of Religious History* (Santa Barbara, CA, 2014), p. 1285.

14 Edward Farrington, *Ernest H. Wilson, Plant Hunter* (Boston, MA, 1931), p. 66.

15 N. Kobayashi et al., 'Chloroplast DNA Polymorphisms and Morphological Variation in Japanese Wild Azaleas, the Origin of Evergreen Azalea Cultivars', *Acta Horticulturae*, DXXI (2000), pp. 173–8.

16 Ernest Henry Wilson and Alfred Rehder, *A Monograph of Azaleas: Rhododendron Subgenus Anthodendron* (Cambridge, 1921), pp. 6–7 and 34–5; C. Ingram, 'Is *Rhododendon kaempferi* a Good Species?', *The Rhododendron and Camellia Yearbook*, X (1956), pp. 28–30.

17 Milne et al., 'A Hybrid Zone Dominated by Fertile F$_1$s'.

18 Milne and Abbott, 'Reproductive Isolation Among Two Interfertile *Rhododendron* Species'.

2 The Fall and Rise of *Azalea*

1 Dr David Chamberlain, pers. comm.

2 Ibid.

3 Chang Chih-Shun et al., 'Notes on Two Ornamentals Cultivated at Yungchhang, Yunnan', cited in Joseph Needham, *Science and Civilisation in China: Biology and Biological Technology, Part 1, Botany* (Cambridge, 1986), vol. VI, p. 438. Needham suggests that the species concerned may include *R. auriculatum*, *R. mucronatum* and *R. pulchrum*.

4 Jakob Breyne, *Prodromus Plantarum* (1860), p. 24, cited in Ernest Wilson and Alfred Rehder, *A Monograph of Azaleas: Rhododendron Subgenus Anthodendron* (Cambridge, 1921), p. 7.

5 John Ray, *Historia Plantarum* (London, 1704), vol. III, pp. 491–2; Wilson and Rehder, *A Monograph of Azaleas*, p. 110.

6 For a time known as *Azalea nudiflora* or *Rhododendron nudiflorum*. This is not the plant now called R. *luteum*.

7 Wilson and Rehder, *A Monograph of Azaleas*, p. 16.

8 John Torrey, *Flora of the Northern and Middle United States* (New York, 1824), vol. I, pp. 423–7.

9 D. F. Chamberlain and S. J. Rae, 'A Revision of *Rhododendron*. IV. Subgenus *Tsutsusi*', *Edinburgh Journal of Botany*, XLVII (1990), pp. 89–200.

10 W. S. Judd and K. A. Kron, 'A Revision of *Rhododendron*. VI. Subgenus *Pentanthera* (sections *Sciadorhodion, Rhodora,* and *Viscidula*)', *Edinburgh Journal of Botany*, LII (1995), pp. 1–54.

11 J. Cullen, 'Naturalised Rhododendrons Widespread in Great Britain and Ireland', *Hanburyana*, V (2011), pp. 11–19; and see Kenneth Cox, 'Why So Called "R. x *superponticum*" is Invalid Taxonomy and Has No Scientific Basis', www.glendoick.com, 1 January 2014.

12 K. A. Kron, 'A Revision of *Rhododendron* Section *Pentanthera*', *Edinburgh Journal of Botany*, L (1993), pp. 249–364.

13 D. F. Chamberlain et al., *The Genus Rhododendron: Its Classification and Synonymy* (Edinburgh, 1996).

14 Y. Kurashige et al., 'Sectional Relationships in the Genus *Rhododendron* (Ericaceae): Evidence from *mat*K and *trn*K Intron Sequences', *Plant Systematics and Evolution*, CCXXVIII (2001), pp. 1–14; L. Goetsch et al., 'The Molecular Systematics of *Rhododendron* (Ericaceae): A Phylogeny Based Upon *RPB2* Gene Sequences', *Systematic Botany*, XXX (2005), pp. 616–26; K. A. Kron, 'Phylogenetic Relationships of Rhododendroideae (Ericaceae)', *American Journal of Botany*, LXXXIV (1997), pp. 973–80. In addition to these, preliminary results from Dr Lianming Gao in Kunming concur with all of the above that *Azalea* is not distinct.

15 Wilson and Rehder, *A Monograph of Azaleas*, p. 17.

16 K. A. Kron and J. M. King, 'Cladistic Relationships of *Kalmia, Leiophyllum,* and *Loiseleuria* (Phyllodoceae, Ericaceae) Based on *rbc*L and nrITS Data', *Systematic Botany*, XXI (1996), pp. 17–29.

17 Donald Hyatt, 'Raising Rhododendrons and Azaleas from Seed', www.tjhsst.edu, accessed 19 September 2015; 'How to Grow and Care for Azalea Bushes', www.gardenersnet.com, accessed 19 September 2015.

18 B. C. Ellery, 'Ghent Hybrid Azaleas are Hardy in New England', *Arnoldia*, III (1943), pp. 37–40; 'Rhododendron: The Hybrids / Azalea Hybrids – Deciduous', www.beanstreesandshrubs.org, accessed 19 September 2015; A. Skinner, 'Rescuing the Ghent and Rustica Flore Pleno Azaleas', *Journal of the American Rhododendron Society*, XXXVIII/3 (1984).

19 Henry Arthur Bright, *A Year in a Victorian Garden* (London, 1989), p. 72.

20 'The Ghent Azalea', www.gentseazalea.be, 2013.

21 Skinner, 'Rescuing the Ghent and Rustica Flore Pleno Azaleas'.

22 Nomad, 'Hardy Azaleas', *Journal of Horticulture*, XXXIII (1877), pp. 449–50.

23 G. D. Waterer, 'Rhododendrons and Azaleas at the Knap Hill Nursery', *Journal of the American Rhododendron Society*, IV/1 (1950).

24 Ibid.

25 R. C. Cash, 'Exbury Azaleas – From History To Your Garden', *Journal of the American Rhododendron Society*, XL/1 (1986).
26 Waterer, 'Rhododendrons and Azaleas at the Knap Hill Nursery'.
27 J. H. Clarke, 'Some Trends in the Development of the Knap Hill Azaleas', *Journal of the American Rhododendron Society*, VI/4 (1952).
28 Waterer, 'Rhododendrons and Azaleas at the Knap Hill Nursery'; Frederick Street, *Hardy Rhododendrons* (London, 1954), p. 36.
29 Waterer, 'Rhododendrons and Azaleas at the Knap Hill Nursery'.
30 P. H. Brydon, 'Exbury Azaleas', *Journal of the American Rhododendron Society*, VIII/4 (1954); Cash, 'Exbury Azaleas'.
31 Clarke, 'Some Trends in the Development of the Knap Hill Azaleas'.
32 G. H. Pinckney, 'The Knap Hill and Exbury strain of Azaleas', *Journal of the American Rhododendron Society*, VII/1 (1953). Mr Pinckney was manager of the Waterer Nursery at Bagshot, then known as John Waterer, Sons & Crisp Ltd.
33 R. Henny, 'Book Review (Hardy Rhododendrons by Frederick Street)', *Journal of the American Rhododendron Society*, VIII/2 (1954).
34 Skinner, 'Rescuing the Ghent and Rustica Flore Pleno Azaleas'.
35 'Rhododendron: The Hybrids / Azalea Hybrids – Deciduous', www.beanstreesandshrubs.org, accessed 19 September 2015.

3 Rhododendromania

1 Frederick Street, *Hardy Rhododendrons* (London, 1954), p. 18.
2 E. H. Wilding, *Index to the Genus Rhododendron* (Stoke Poges, 1920).
3 Alice Coats, *The Quest For Plants* (London, 1969), p. 149.
4 Deepak Kumar, 'Botanical Exploration and The East India Company', in *The East India Company and the Natural World*, ed. Vinita Damodaran et al. (Basingstoke, 2014), p. 26.
5 Coats, *The Quest For Plants*, p. 149; Kumar, 'Botanical Exploration and The East India Company', p. 27.
6 Coats, *The Quest For Plants*, p. 149.
7 Ibid., pp. 149–50.
8 W. H. Lang, 'William Griffith, 1810–1845', in *Makers of British Botany: A Collection of Biographies by Living Botanists*, ed. Francis W. Oliver (Cambridge, 1913), p. 179 (of 178–91).
9 Coats, *The Quest For Plants*, p. 153.
10 Ibid.
11 W. and R. Chambers, 'Mr Bruce's Report on Assam Tea', *Chambers Edinburgh Journal*, II–III/417 (1840), pp. 2–3.
12 Coats, *The Quest For Plants*, p. 153.
13 Ibid., p. 154.
14 Ibid.
15 Frank Kingdon-Ward, 'Botanical Exploration in the Mishmi Hills', *Himalayan Journal*, 1 (1929).
16 Lang, 'William Griffith, 1810–1845', p. 181.

17 Coats, *The Quest For Plants*, p. 154.
18 Lang, 'William Griffith, 1810–1845', p. 181.
19 Euan Cox, *Plant Hunting in China* (London, 1945), pp. 70–71.
20 Robert Fortune, *Three Years of Wandering in the Northern Provinces of China* (London, 1847), p. 392 onwards; Sarah Rose, *For All the Tea in China: Espionage, Empire and the Secret Formula for the World's Favourite Drink* (London, 2013), pp. 17–21.
21 Rose, *For All the Tea in China*; Toby Musgrave et al., *The Plant Hunters* (London, 1999), pp. 119–21.
22 Fortune, *Three Years of Wandering in the Northern Provinces of China*; Rose, *For All the Tea in China*, p. 16.
23 Cox, *Plant Hunting in China*, pp. 82–9.
24 Joseph Hooker, *Himalayan Journals: Notes of a Naturalist*, 1999 edn (New Delhi, 1999), vol. I, p. 117.
25 Ray Desmond, *Sir Joseph Dalton Hooker, Traveller and Plant Collector* (Woodbridge, 1998), pp. 122–9. vol. I, pp. 285, 300 and elsewhere.
26 Ibid., pp. 292–3.
27 Ibid., p. 295.
28 'Pre-Independence', www.darjeeling.gov.in, accessed 19 September 2015.
29 Leonard Huxley, ed., *The Life and Letters of Sir Joseph Dalton Hooker* (London, 1918), vol. I, pp. 309–10.
30 Desmond, *Sir Joseph Dalton Hooker*, p. 155.
31 Huxley, *The Life and Letters of Sir Joseph Dalton Hooker*, vol. I, p. 313.
32 Hooker, *Himalayan Journals*, vol. II, p. 209.
33 Musgrave et al., *The Plant Hunters*, p. 96.
34 Ibid., pp. 83–96.
35 Huxley, *The Life and Letters of Sir Joseph Dalton Hooker*, vol. I, p. 313.
36 Musgrave et al., *The Plant Hunters*, p. 97.
37 Joseph Hooker, *Rhododendrons of the Sikkim Himalayas* (London, 1849–51). Published as two volumes.
38 Desmond, *Sir Joseph Dalton Hooker*, p. 274.
39 Street, *Hardy Rhododendrons*, p. 72.
40 Ibid., pp. 72 and 34.
41 Ibid., pp. 79 and 69.
42 Sue Shephard and Tony Musgrave, *Blue Orchid and Big Tree* (Bristol, 2014), p. 81.
43 Street, *Hardy Rhododendrons*, pp. 39–40.
44 '*Rhododendron* "Britannia"', www.hirsutum.info, accessed 19 September 2015.
45 Street, *Hardy Rhododendrons*, p. 54; Diana Wells, *100 Flowers and How They Got Their Names* (Chapel Hill, NC, 1997), p. 200.
46 Street, *Hardy Rhododendrons*, p. 52.
47 Judith Taylor, *Visions of Loveliness: Great Flower Breeders of the Past* (Athens, OH, 2014), p. 130.
48 Street, *Hardy Rhododendrons*, pp. 53–5.
49 'HL Deb 26 November 1963 vol 253 cc606–33', http://hansard.millbanksystems.com, 26 November 1963.

50 Street, *Hardy Rhododendrons*, p. 52.

51 C. L. Justice, 'The Victorian Rhododendron Story', *Journal of the American Rhododendron Society*, LIII/3 (1999). Justice attributes this quote to Germaine Greer's 'Rose Blight' pseudonym, under which she wrote 34 columns for *Private Eye* magazine between 1978 and 1979; however, none of these contain this particular quote.

52 Street, *Hardy Rhododendrons*, pp. 56–7.

53 This is based on an analysis on the recorded hybrids involving each species, directly and indirectly, on website www.hirsutum.info, accessed during August 2015.

54 Griffith discovered *griffithianum*, but Hooker introduced it.

55 Bean, *Trees and Shrubs Hardy in the British Isles*, p. 348.

56 For example, 'How We Propagate our Plants', www.rhododendrons.co.uk, accessed 19 September 2015.

57 '*Rhododendron campylocarpum* ssp *campylocarpum*', www.hirsutum.info, accessed 19 September 2015.

58 Street, *Hardy Rhododendrons*, p. 37.

59 Wilding, *Index to the Genus Rhododendron*, 1920.

60 Charles Williams, 'RHS Lecture – "The Smellies"', www.caerhays.co.uk, accessed 19 September 2015.

61 There are two supposed exceptions to this rule, but neither is a good garden plant, and the current author is sceptical of their true parentage.

62 Williams, 'RHS Lecture – "The Smellies"', www.caerhays.co.uk, accessed 19 September 2015.

63 James Veitch & Sons Ltd, *Catalogue of Plants* (London, 1869), p. 54.

64 Williams, 'RHS Lecture – "The Smellies"', www.caerhays.co.uk, accessed 19 September 2015; Abbie Jury, 'Fragrant Rhododendrons', www.jury.co.nz, 6 July 2012.

65 '*Rhododendron* "Praecox"', www.hirsutum.info, accessed 19 September 2015; Street, *Hardy Rhododendrons*, p. 67.

66 '*Rhododendron ciliatum*', www.hirsutum.info, accessed 19 September 2015.

67 C. J. Hebert et al., '*In Vitro* Regeneration of *Rhododendron* "Fragrantissimum Improved"', *SNA Research Conference*, LIV (2009), pp. 460–63.

68 Francis Kingdon-Ward et al., *Frank Kingdon Ward's Riddle of the Tsangpo Gorges: Retracing the Epic Journey of 1924–25 in South-East Tibet*, 2nd edn (Woodbridge, 2008), p. 148.

69 Information available at www.hirsutum.info, accessed 19 September 2015.

70 G. Bell, 'Halfdan Lem, Hybridizer', *Journal of the American Rhododendron Society*, XXXI/1 (1977).

71 Susan Stamberg, 'Impressionist Hero Edouard Manet Gets The Star Treatment In Los Angeles', www.npr.org, 27 February 2015.

72 'Mauveine – The Discovery and Inventor', www.rsc.org, accessed 19 September 2015.

73 'The Mauve Measles', *Punch Magazine* (20 August 1859), p. 81.

74 'The Story of the *Rhododendron niveum*', www.heligan.com, accessed 19 September 2015.

4 Glasshouse Sensations

1 Sue Shephard, *Seeds of Fortune: A Gardening Dynasty* (London, 2003), pp. 1–30; James Herbert Veitch, *Hortus Veitchii: A History of the Rise and Progress of the Nurseries of Messrs. James Veitch and Sons, together with an Account of the Botanical Collectors and Hybridists Employed by them and a List of the Most Remarkable of their Introductions* (London, 1906), p. 8.

2 Shephard, *Seeds of Fortune*, pp. 15–30.

3 Ibid., pp. 30 and 39–40.

4 Ibid., pp. 45 and 63; Veitch, *Hortus Veitchii*, p. 99.

5 Ray Desmond, *Kew: The History of the Royal Botanic Gardens* (London, 1998), pp. 127–49.

6 Henry Hobhouse, *Seeds of Change*, 4th edn (London, 1999), pp. 26–7.

7 Desmond, *Kew*, p. 156 onwards; Shephard, *Seeds of Fortune*, pp. 42, 71.

8 Toby Musgrave et al., *The Plant Hunters* (London, 1999), p. 21.

9 Shephard, *Seeds of Fortune*, p. 74.

10 Veitch, *Hortus Veitchii*, p. 37; Sue Shephard and Toby Musgrave, *Blue Orchid and Big Tree* (Bristol, 2014), pp. 22–3.

11 Veitch, *Hortus Veitchii*, pp. 38–9.

12 W. Magor, 'A History of Rhododendrons', *Journal of the American Rhododendron Society*, XLIV/4 (1990).

13 Shephard and Musgrave, *Blue Orchid and Big Tree*, pp. 42–6.

14 George Argent, *Rhododendrons of Subgenus Vireya* (London, 2006), p. 121.

15 Veitch, *Hortus Veitchii*, p. 42; Shephard and Musgrave, *Blue Orchid and Big Tree*, p. 50.

16 Joseph Hooker, *Himalayan Journals: Notes of a Naturalist*, 1999 edn (New Delhi, 1999), vol. II, p. 242.

17 Veitch, *Hortus Veitchii*, p. 448; Toby Musgrave et al., *The Plant Hunters*, p. 146.

18 Veitch, *Hortus Veitchii*, pp. 99–101, 106–9 and 86.

19 G. Henslow, 'Hybrid Rhododendrons', *Journal of the Royal Horticultural Society*, VIII (1891), pp. 240–830.

20 Ibid., p. 241.

21 Ibid., p. 247.

22 Ibid., p. 269.

23 Ibid., p. 241.

24 Based on all crosses described in Henslow, 'Hybrid Rhododendrons'.

25 Henslow, 'Hybrid Rhododendrons', p. 250.

26 Ibid. pp. 256–8, 257 and 255.

27 Veitch, *Hortus Veitchii*, p. 27.

28 Shephard, *Seeds of Fortune*, p. 81.

29 Veitch, *Hortus Veitchii*, p. 27.

30 Shephard, *Seeds of Fortune*, pp. 167–8.

31 Veitch, *Hortus Veitchii*, pp. 37–44.

32 Ibid., pp. 49–50; Shephard, *Seeds of Fortune*, p. 169.

33 Veitch, *Hortus Veitchii*, p. 27; Shephard, *Seeds of Fortune*, p. 194.

34 Veitch, *Hortus Veitchii*, p. 91.

35 Chris Callard, 'The History of Vireya Rhododendron Culture', www.vireya.net, 28 January 2015.

36 Shephard, *Seeds of Fortune*, pp. 258, 273.

37 Protheroe and Morris, 'A Catalogue of the First Portion of the Unusually Well-grown Nursery Stock Cultivated with so much Success at this Famous Nursery, and in Which Will be Found Examples of the Varieties from Messrs. J. VEITCH & SONS' Unique Collection of New and Rare Plants' (London, 1913).

38 'In Memoriam. James Leonard Veitch', *Kew Guild Journal*, III/26 (1919), www.kewguild.org.uk; 'John Leonard Veitch', www.cwgc.org, accessed 18 February 2016. Despite the different names, these clearly refer to the same man.

39 Shephard, *Seeds of Fortune*, p. 279; 'Anna Mildred Veitch (1889–1969)', www.devongardenstrust.org.uk, accessed 19 September 2015; Caradoc Doy, 'Veitch Family History', www.stbridgetnurseries.co.uk, accessed 19 September 2015.

40 Chris Callard, 'Vireya Hybrid Lists', www.vireya.net, 28 January 2015.

41 Argent, *Rhododendrons of Subgenus Vireya*.

42 G. K. Brown et al., 'Phylogeny of *Rhododendron* Section *Vireya* (Ericaceae) Based on Two Non-coding Regions of cpDNA', *Plant Systematics and Evolution*, CCLVII (2006), pp. 57–93; L. A. Goetsch et al., 'Major Speciation Accompanied the Dispersal of Vireya Rhododendrons (Ericaceae, *Rhododendron* sect. *Schistanthe*) through the Malayan Archipelago: Evidence from Nuclear Gene Sequences', *Taxon*, LX (2011), pp. 1015–28.

43 Argent, *Rhododendrons of Subgenus Vireya*.

44 Ibid.

45 Goetsch et al., 'Major Speciation Accompanied the Dispersal of Vireya Rhododendrons'.

46 Ronald Blakey, 'Paleogeographic Globes – Miocene', www2.nau.edu, accessed 19 September 2015.

47 Section *Vireya* (or *Schistanthe*) of subgenus *Rhododendron*. The only non-vireyas anywhere on the archipelago are two members of *Hymenanthes* in Sumatra.

5 The Home of the Rhododendrons

1 Euan Cox, *Plant Hunting in China* (London, 1945), p. 68.

2 Ibid., pp. 98–100, 138. Yichang was sometimes called Ichang.

3 James Herbert Veitch, *Hortus Veitchii: A History of the Rise and Progress of the Nurseries of Messrs. James Veitch and Sons, together with an Account of the Botanical Collectors and Hybridists Employed by them and a List of the Most Remarkable of their Introductions* (London, 1906), pp. 96 and 138.

4 Cox, *Plant Hunting in China*, pp. 112–15; 'Père David – Jean Pierre Armand David (1826–1900)', www.plantexplorers.com, accessed 19 September 2015.

5 Ibid.

6 W. Magor, 'A History of Rhododendrons', *Journal of the American Rhododendron Society*, XLIV/4 (1990).

7 Adrien Franchat, *Plantae Delavayanae. Plantes de Chine recueillies au Yunnan par l'Abbé Delavay* (Paris, 1889).

8 Cox, *Plant Hunting in China*, pp. 115–18; 'Père Jean Marie Delavay (1834–1895)', www.plantexplorers.com, accessed 19 September 2015.

9 Cox, *Plant Hunting in China*, pp. 119–20; 'Père Paul Guillaume Farges (1844–1912)', www.plantexplorers.com, accessed 19 September 2015.

10 Seamus O'Brien, *In the Footsteps of Augustine Henry* (Woodbridge, 2011), p. 233.

11 Roy W. Briggs, *'Chinese' Wilson: A Life of Ernest H. Wilson, 1876–1930* (London, 1993).

12 Cox, *Plant Hunting in China*, p. 138.

13 Toby Musgrave et al., *The Plant Hunters* (London, 1999), pp. 157–8.

14 Briggs, *'Chinese' Wilson*, pp. 20–23.

15 Ibid., pp. 23–4.

16 Ibid., p. 29.

17 Ibid., pp. 60–73.

18 Ibid., p. 73.

19 Musgrave et al., *The Plant Hunters*, p. 171.

20 Edward Farrington, *Ernest H. Wilson, Plant Hunter* (Boston, MA, 1931), p. 66; and see Chapter One.

21 See pictures in Briggs, *'Chinese' Wilson*, pp. 80 and 91–2, and judge for yourself.

22 Ernest Wilson and Alfred Rehder, *A Monograph of Azaleas: Rhododendron Subgenus Anthodendron* (Cambridge, 1921).

23 Briggs, *'Chinese' Wilson*; Cox, *Plant Hunting in China*, p. 150.

24 Cox, *Plant Hunting in China*, pp. 173–6.

25 Ibid., pp. 177–8.

26 Ibid., p. 177.

27 The two books are called *On the Eaves of the World* (London, 1917) and *The Rainbow Bridge* (London, 1921).

28 Cox, *Plant Hunting in China*, pp. 178–9.

29 R. E. Cooper et al., eds, *George Forrest, V.M.H., 1873–1932* (Haddington, 1935), p. 11; Brenda McLean, *George Forrest, Plant Hunter* (Woodbridge, 2004), p. 22.

30 Musgrave et al., *The Plant Hunters*, p. 178. Forrest learned specimen making during training at an apothecary, and had taken part in Australia's gold rush, though not very successfully.

31 Bulley ran Bees Ltd Nurseries, and had a particular fondness for *Primula*, making this genus the initial focus of Forrest's collecting activities. Bulley and Forrest fell out over money during Forrest's second expedition.

32 Musgrave et al., *The Plant Hunters*, p. 181.

33 Ibid.

34 Cox, *Plant Hunting in China*, pp. 119–20.

35 Musgrave et al., *The Plant Hunters*, p. 184.

36 Ibid.; Cooper et al., *George Forrest*, pp. 31–2.

37 Cooper et al., *George Forrest*, pp. 31–7.

38 Ibid., p. 33.

39 Brenda McLean, *George Forrest, Plant Hunter*, p. 70.

40 Erik Mueggler, *The Paper Road: Archive and Experience in the Botanical Exploration of West China and Tibet* (Berkeley, CA, and London, 2011), p. 23.

41 Cooper et al., *George Forrest*, pp. 33–4.

42 Ibid., p. 22; Mueggler, *The Paper Road*, p. 142.

43 'George Forrest (1873–1932)', www.plantexplorers.com, accessed 19 September 2015.

44 Mueggler, *The Paper Road*, pp. 8–9, 46.

45 E. H. Wilding, *Index to the Genus Rhododendron* (Stoke Poges, 1920).

46 Cooper et al., *George Forrest*, p. 83; Mueggler, *The Paper Road*, pp. 24, 34, 127–30 and note 39.

47 Mueggler, *The Paper Road*, pp. 114, 119, 143 and others.

48 McLean, *George Forrest, Plant Hunter*, p. 145.

49 'George Forrest (1873–1932)', www.plantexplorers.com.

50 McLean, *George Forrest, Plant Hunter*, pp. 185–8.

51 Musgrave et al., *The Plant Hunters*, p. 193.

52 K. C. Nixon and W. L. Crepet, 'Late Cretaceous Fossil Flowers of Ericalean Affinity', *American Journal of Botany*, LXXX (1993), pp. 616–23.

53 S. E. Smith and D. J. Read, *Mycorrhizal Symbiosis*, 3rd edn (London, 2008).

54 W. Tian et al., 'Diversity of Culturable Ericoid Mycorrhizal Fungi of *Rhododendron decorum* in Yunnan, China', *Mycologia*, CIII (2011), pp. 703–9.

55 D. J. Read and J. Perez-Moreno, 'Mycorrhizas and Nutrient Cycling in Ecosystems – A Journey Towards Relevance?', *New Phytologist*, CLVII (2003), pp. 475–92; J.W.G. Cairney and A. A. Meharg, 'Ericoid Mycorrhiza: A Partnership that Exploits Harsh Edaphic Conditions', *European Journal of Soil Science*, LIV (2003), pp. 735–40; J. Cornelissen et al., 'Carbon Cycling Traits of Plant Species are Linked with Mycorrhizal Strategy', *Oecologia*, CXXIX (2001), pp. 611–19.

56 Cooper et al., *George Forrest*, p. 71.

57 R. Zetter and M. Hesse, 'The Morphology of Pollen Tetrads and Viscin Threads in Some Tertiary, *Rhododendron*-like Ericaceae', *Grana*, XXXV (1996), pp. 286–94.

58 Y. Kurashige et al., 'Sectional Relationships in the Genus *Rhododendron* (Ericaceae): Evidence from *mat*K and *trn*K Intron Sequences', *Plant Systematics and Evolution*, CCXXVIII (2001), pp. 1–14; L. Goetsch et al., 'The Molecular Systematics of *Rhododendron* (Ericaceae): A Phylogeny Based Upon *RPB2* Gene Sequences', *Systematic Botany*, XXX (2005), pp. 616–26; Lianming Gao, unpublished data.

59 Dates showing when subgenus *Rhododendron* diverged from *Hymenanthes* come from R. I. Milne, 'Phylogeny and Biogeography of *Rhododendron* Subsection *Pontica*, a Group with a Tertiary Relict Distribution', *Molecular Phylogenetics and Evolution*, XXXIII (2004), pp. 389–401. *Tsutsusi* might have branched off earlier: Kurashige et al., 'Sectional

Relationships in the Genus *Rhododendron*'; Goetsch et al., 'The Molecular Systematics of *Rhododendron*'; K. A. Kron, 'Phylogenetic Relationships of Rhododendroideae (Ericaceae)', *American Journal of Botany*, LXXXIV (1997), pp. 973–80.

60 Milne, 'Phylogeny and Biogeography of *Rhododendron* Subsection *Pontica*'.

61 R. I. Milne, 'Northern Hemisphere Plant Disjunctions: A Window on Tertiary Land Bridges and Climate Change?', *Annals of Botany*, XCVIII (2006), pp. 465–72.

62 Milne, 'Phylogeny and Biogeography of *Rhododendron* Subsection *Pontica*'.

63 T. M. Harrison et al., 'Raising Tibet', *Science*, CCLV (1992), pp. 1663–70.

64 Milne, 'Phylogeny and Biogeography of *Rhododendron* Subsection *Pontica*'.

65 McLean, *George Forrest, Plant Hunter*, p. 141.

66 Hannah Wilson, unpublished data; R. I. Milne et al., 'Phylogeny of *Rhododendron* Subgenus *Hymenanthes* Based on Chloroplast DNA Markers: Between-lineage Hybridisation During Adaptive Radiation?', *Plant Systematics and Evolution*, CCLXXXV (2010), pp. 233–44.

67 Dr David Chamberlain, pers. comm.

68 Cox, *Plant Hunting in China*, pp. 181–3, gives a neat chronological summary up to 1939; and see Musgrave et al., *The Plant Hunters*, pp. 199–215.

69 Cox, *Plant Hunting in China*, pp. 180–89.

70 Musgrave et al., *The Plant Hunters*, pp. 202–13.

71 Ibid., p. 215.

72 Francis Kingdon-Ward et al., *Frank Kingdon Ward's Riddle of the Tsangpo Gorges: Retracing the Epic Journey of 1924–25 in South-east Tibet*, 2nd edn (Woodbridge, 2008), p. 148.

73 Ibid., pp. 201–11.

74 Jean Kingdon-Ward, *My Hill So Strong* (London, 1952).

75 Frank Kingdon-Ward, 'The Kingdon Ward Expedition to Assam', *Journal of the American Rhododendron Society*, V/1 (1951).

76 Musgrave et al., *The Plant Hunters*, p. 215.

77 'Yu, Te-Tsun (1908–1986)', https://plants.jstor.org, 19 April 2013.

78 De-Yuan Hong and Stephen Blackmore, eds, *The Plants of China* (Cambridge, 2015).

79 Weng Pei Fang, '*Rhododendron youngiae*', *Contributions from the Biological Laboratory of the Science Society of China. Botanical Series*, XII (1939), p. 24.

80 Mueggler, *The Paper Road*, p. 16.

81 Dr David Chamberlain, pers. comm.

82 Ibid.

83 Peter Cox and Peter Hutchison, *Seeds of Adventure: In Search of Plants* (Woodbridge, 2008).

84 Dr David Chamberlain, pers. comm.

85 Ibid.

86 'Gao Lianming's Group', http://english.kib.cas.cn, accessed 19 September 2015.

87 See 'Publications Authored by Jianquan Liu', www.pubfacts.com, accessed 19 September 2015.

6 Potions, Petals and Poisons

1 A. Dampc and M. Luczkiewicz, 'Rhododendron tomentosum (Ledum palustre). A Review of Traditional Use Based on Current Research', *Fitoterapia*, LXXXV (2013), pp. 130–43.

2 Adrienne Mayor, 'Mithradates: Scourge of Rome', *History Today*, LIX (2009), pp. 10–15.

3 'The Pontos Kingdom', www.kultur.gov.tr, accessed 19 September 2015.

4 Adrienne Mayor, 'Mad Honey!', *Archaeology*, XLVIII (1995), pp. 32–40.

5 Anja These et al., 'A Case of Human Poisoning by Grayanotoxins Following Honey Ingestion: Elucidation of the Toxin Profile by Mass Spectrometry', *Food Additives & Contaminants: Part A*, XXXII (2015), pp. 1674–84.

6 Mayor, 'Mad Honey!'; Laïd Boukraâ, *Honey in Traditional and Modern Medicine* (Boca Raton, FL, 2013), p. 396.

7 Mayor, 'Mithradates: Scourge of Rome'.

8 D. Leach, 'That's Why the Lady is a Tramp', *Journal of the American Rhododendron Society*, XXXVI/4 (1982).

9 S. A. Jansen et al., 'Grayanotoxin Poisoning: "Mad Honey Disease" and Beyond', *Cardiovascular Toxicology*, XII (2012), pp. 208–15.

10 Xenophon, *Anabasis*, book 4, pp. 820–21.

11 H. Demir et al., 'Mad Honey Intoxication: A Case Series of 21 Patients', *ISRN Toxicology* (2011), article ID 526426.

12 Jansen et al., 'Grayanotoxin Poisoning'; Mayor, 'Mad Honey!'.

13 These et al., 'A Case of Human Poisoning by Grayanotoxins'; Demir et al., 'Mad Honey Intoxication'.

14 Joseph Hooker, *Himalayan Journals: Notes of a Naturalist*, 1999 edn (New Delhi, 1999), vol. I, p. 201; Matt, 'Raw Honey Almost Killed Me!!!!', www.bees-and-beekeeping.com, accessed 19 September 2015.

15 Demir et al., 'Mad Honey Intoxication'; 'Ever Heard of Mad Honey?' www.hehasawifeyouknow.tumblr.com, 8 May 2012.

16 Laïd Boukraâ, *Honey in Traditional and Modern Medicine*, p. 396. *Kalmia*, and/or *Rhododendron*, might account for the Seattle incident.

17 Mayor, 'Mad Honey!'

18 Ibid.; Hooker, *Himalayan Journals*, vol. I, p. 201.

19 Mayor, 'Mad Honey!'

20 E. Georgian and E. Emshwiller, '*Rhododendron* Uses and Distribution of this Knowledge within Ethnic Groups in Northwest Yunnan Province, China', *Open Journal of Social Sciences*, IV (2016), pp. 138–50.

21 Council of Scientific and Industrial Research, *The Wealth of India* (New Delhi, 1972), vol. IX, p. 14.

22 A. Paul et al., 'Utilization of Rhododendrons by Monpas in Western Arunachal Pradesh, India', *Journal of the American Rhododendron Society*, LXIV/2 (2010).

23 Narayan Mahanandar, *Plants and People of Nepal* (Portland, OR, 2002), p. 395; Pooja Bhula, 'Buransh: The Delicious and Intoxicating Rhododendron Juice of Uttarakhand', www.dnaindia.com, 20 February 2014.

24 A. D. Kharwal and D. S. Rawat, 'Ethnobotanical Studies and Distribution of Different *Rhododendron* Species in Himachal Pradesh, India', *Plant Sciences Feed*, III (2013), pp. 46–9; Mahanandar, *Plants and People of Nepal*, p. 394.

25 Bhula, 'Buransh: The Delicious and Intoxicating Rhododendron Juice of Uttarakhand', www.dnaindia.com.

26 Karen Coates, 'Rhododendron Wine', www.ramblingspoon.com, 19 January 2008; David Chamberlain, pers. comm.

27 Council of Scientific and Industrial Research, *The Wealth of India* reports this, but expresses doubt about its veracity.

28 S. P. Ambasta et al., *The Useful Plants of India* (New Delhi, 1986), p. 522.

29 Jansen et al., 'Grayanotoxin Poisoning'.

30 S. M. Jeong et al., 'A Case of Systemic Toxicity that Occurred in an Adult who Intentionally Ingested *Rhododendron schlippenbachii*', *Journal of Korean Society and Clinical Toxicology*, VII (2009), pp. 180–82.

31 Toby Musgrave et al., *The Plant Hunters* (London, 1999), p. 202.

32 W. Klein-Schwartz and T. Litovitz, 'Azalea Toxicity: An Overrated Problem?', *Journal of Toxicology: Clinical Toxicology*, XXIII (1985), pp. 91–101.

33 Dr Rebecca Yahr, Royal Botanic Garden, Edinburgh, pers. comm.; Leach, 'That's Why the Lady is a Tramp'.

34 Jean Bruneton, *Toxic Plants Dangerous to Humans and Animals* (Andover, 1999), p. 254.

35 L. M. Milewski and S. F. Kahn, 'An Overview of Potentially Life-threatening Poisonous Plants in Dogs and Cats', *Journal of Veterinary Emergency and Critical Care*, XVI (2006), pp. 25–33.

36 V. Beasley, 'Andromedotoxin (Grayanotoxin) - Containing plants (Heath, Ericaceae plant family)', in *Veterinary Toxicology*, ed. V. Beasley (Ithaca, NY, 1999); Bruneton, *Toxic Plants Dangerous to Humans and Animals*, p. 254; Leach, 'That's Why the Lady is a Tramp'.

37 Marianna Kneller, *The Book of Rhododendrons* (Newton Abbott, 1995), p. 104.

38 Pat Halliday, *The Illustrated Rhododendron: Their Classification Portrayed Through the Artwork of Curtis's Botanical Magazine* (London, 2001), p. 126.

39 I. Hough, 'Rhododendron Poisoning in a Western Gray Kangaroo', *Australian Veterinary Journal*, LXXV (1997), pp. 174–5; J. E. Crawford, 'Rhododendron Poisoning in Alpacas (Correspondence)', *Veterinary Record*, CXLIV (1999), p. 680; R. M. Miller, 'Azalea Poisoning in a Llama: A Case Report', *Veterinary Medicine, Small Animal Clinician*, LXXVI (1981), p. 104; Sérgio Farias Vargas Junior et al., '*Rhododendron simsii* Poisoning in Goats in Southern Brazil', *Ciência Rural*, XLIV (2014), pp. 1249–52.

40 D. H. Black, 'Rhododendron Poisoning in Sheep', *Veterinary Record*, LXXVIII (1991), pp. 363–4.

41 Ryan Douglas, University of Edinburgh, pers. comm.; S. Casteel and
J. Wagstaff, 'Rhododendron macrophyllum Poisoning in a Group of Goats
and Sheep', Veterinary and Human Toxicology, XXXI (1989), pp. 176–7.
42 Aly Balsom, 'Sheep Farmers Warned about Rhododendron Poisoning',
www.fwi.co.uk, 8 December 2010.
43 Ryan Douglas, University of Edinburgh, pers. comm.
44 'Rhododendron Poisoning', http://blog.tarset.co.uk, 6 January 2010;
Irene Ramsay and Lorraine, 'Poisonous Plant Antidotes',
www.goatworld.com, accessed 19 September 2015; Molly Nolte,
'Goat Medications: Natural & Alternative Treatments & Medicines',
https://fiascofarm.com, p. 3, accessed 19 September 2015; David
Mackenzie, Goat Husbandry (London, 2011).
45 Mahanandar, Plants and People of Nepal, p. 395.
46 Rebecca Pradhan, 'Wild Rhododendrons of Bhutan', in Rhododendrons
in Horticulture and Science, ed. G. Argent and M. McFarlane (Edinburgh,
2003), pp. 37–41.
47 R. Sõukand et al., 'Uninvited Guests: Traditional Insect Repellents in
Estonia Used Against the Clothes Moth Tineola Bisselliella, Human Flea
Pulex Irritons and Bedbug Cimex Lectularius', Journal of Insect Science, X (2010),
article 150; Manuel Pardo-de-Santayana et al., Ethnobotany in the New
Europe: People, Health and Wild Plant Resources (Oxford and Brooklyn, NY,
2010), pp. 274–6; 'Rahvapärased taimenimetused: Sookail' and
'Rahvapärased taimenimetused: Sookael', http://herba.folklore.ee,
accessed 22 September 2015 (translated from Estonian).
48 Dampc and Luczkiewicz, 'Rhododendron tomentosum (Ledum palustre)'.
49 Ibid.
50 James A. Klocke et al., 'Grayanoid Diterpene Insect Antifeedants
and Insecticides from Rhododendron molle', Phytochemistry, XXX (1991),
pp. 1797–800; G. H. Zhong et al., 'Studies on Extracts of Rhododendron
molle as Oviposition Deterrentants and Ovicides against Plutella xylostella
L. (Lepidoptera: Plutellklae)', Journal of South China Agricultural University,
XXI (2000), pp. 40–43.
51 Ambasta et al., The Useful Plants of India, pp. 519–20; Pradhan, 'Wild
Rhododendrons of Bhutan', pp. 37–41.
52 Georgian and Emshwiller, 'Rhododendron Uses'.
53 Kent Lightfoot and Otis Parish, California Indians and Their Environment
(Berkeley, CA, 2009), p. 231.
54 Council of Scientific and Industrial Research, The Wealth of India, pp. 14–16;
C. Justice, 'Sikkim Experiences', Journal of the American Rhododendron Society,
XLVI/1 (1992); Hooker, Himalayan Journals, vol. II, p. 150.
55 Pradhan, 'Wild Rhododendrons of Bhutan', pp. 37–41.
56 Mahanandar, Plants and People of Nepal, p. 395; A.R.K. Satry and P. K. Hadra,
Rhododendrons in India: Floral & Foliar Splendour of the Himalayan Flora
(Hyderabad, 2010), p. 8.
57 'A History of the Rhododendron Festival', www.rhodyfestival.org,
accessed 19 September 2015; 'Native Plants Associated with Sudden Oak

Death (SOD) and their use by California Indians – Fact Sheet No. 14',
www.suddenoakdeath.org, accessed 19 September 2015.

58 Erik Mueggler, *The Paper Road: Archive and Experience in the Botanical Exploration of West China and Tibet* (Berkeley, CA, and London, 2011).

59 Ibid., p. 109.

60 Ibid., pp. 109–10.

61 Ibid., pp. 112–13 and 305 (note 52).

62 Ibid., p. 119.

63 Georgian and Emshwiller, 'Rhododendron Uses'.

64 Ibid.

65 E. Dilber et al., 'A Case of Mad Honey Poisoning Presenting with Convulsion: Intoxication Instead of Alternative Therapy', *Turkish Journal of Medical Science*, XXXII (2002), pp. 361–2.

66 'Buransh Juice', www.honeyphondaghat.in, accessed 19 September 2015; Ambasta et al., *The Useful Plants of India*, p. 521; Mahanandar, *Plants and People of Nepal*, pp. 394–5; Bhula, 'Buransh: The Delicious and Intoxicating Rhododendron Juice of Uttarakhand', www.dnaindia.com.

67 Kharwal and Rawat, 'Ethnobotanical Studies and Distribution of Different *Rhododendron* Species in Himachal Pradesh'; Mahanandar, *Plants and People of Nepal*, pp. 394–5; Ambasta et al., *The Useful Plants of India*, pp. 519–20.

68 Pradhan, 'Wild Rhododendrons of Bhutan', pp. 37–41.

69 Mahanandar, *Plants and People of Nepal*, p. 396.

70 Ambasta et al., *The Useful Plants of India*, pp. 519–20.

71 Kharwal and Rawat, 'Ethnobotanical Studies and Distribution of Different *Rhododendron* Species in Himachal Pradesh'.

72 Mahanandar, *Plants and People of Nepal*, pp. 394–6.

73 A. P. Colak et al., '*Rhododendron ponticum* in Native and Exotic Environments, with Particular Reference to Turkey and the British Isles', *Journal of Practical Ecology and Conservation*, II (1998), pp. 34–41.

74 Dilber et al., 'A Case of Mad Honey Poisoning Presenting with Convulsion'; Colak et al., '*Rhododendron ponticum* in Native and Exotic Environments'; I. Koca and A. F. Koca, 'Poisoning by Mad Honey: A Brief Review', *Food and Chemical Toxicology*, XLV (2007), pp. 1315–18; Bruneton, *Toxic Plants Dangerous to Humans and Animals*, p. 251.

75 Dilber et al., 'A Case of Mad Honey Poisoning Presenting with Convulsion'.

76 W. T. Poon et al., 'Grayanotoxin Poisoning from *Rhododendron simsii* in an Infant', *Hong Kong Medical Journal*, XIV (2008), pp. 405–7.

77 A. J. Kim et al., 'Grayanotoxin Intoxication – 3 Case Reports', *Journal of the Korean Society of Emergency Medicine*, XI (2000), pp. 372–7.

78 Harvey Felter and John Lloyd, *King's American Dispensatory* (Cincinnati, OH, 1905), pp. 1124–5.

79 Dampc and Luczkiewicz, '*Rhododendron tomentosum* (*Ledum palustre*)'.

80 Pardo-de-Santayana et al., *Ethnobotany in the New Europe*, pp. 274–6.

81 'Rahvapärased taimenimetused: Sookail', http://herba.folklore.ee, accessed 22 September 2015; Charles F. Millspaugh, *American Medicinal*

Plants: An Illustrated and Descriptive Guide to Plants Indigenous to and Naturalized in the United States which are Used in Medicine (North Chelmsford, MA, 1892), p. 392.

82 'Rahvapärased taimenimetused: Sookail', 'Rahvapärased taimenimetused: Sookael' and 'Rahvapärased taimenimetused: Kailud', http://herba.folklore.ee, accessed 22 September 2015.

83 Dampc and Luczkiewicz, '*Rhododendron tomentosum* (*Ledum palustre*)'.

84 Ibid.

85 Georgi Viktorov, pers. comm.

86 Stephen Buhner, *Sacred and Herbal Healing Beers: The Secrets of Ancient Fermentation* (Boulder, CO, 1998), pp. 167 and 169.

87 Ibid., pp. 180–82.

88 Millspaugh, *American Medicinal Plants*, p. 392; James Johnson, *The Chemistry of Common Life* (New York, 1855), p. 55; Buhner, *Sacred and Herbal Healing Beers*, p. 181.

89 'Rahvapärased taimenimetused: Sookail', http://herba.folklore.ee, accessed 22 September 2015.

90 Clive Stace, *New Flora of the British Isles*, 3rd edn (Cambridge, 2010), p. 526.

91 Buhner, *Sacred and Herbal Healing Beers*, p. 173.

92 Johnson, *The Chemistry of Common Life*, p. 55.

93 Stephen H. Buhner, 'The Fall of Gruit and the Rise of Brewer's Droop', now www.gaianstudies.org, 2003.

7 The Tears of the Cuckoo

1 'Dujuan Hua/Azalea', http://castleofcostamesa.com, accessed 19 September 2015.

2 Feng Guomei, *Rhododendrons of China* (Beijing, 1988), vol. 1, p. 3.

3 Dr Wu Zengyuan, Kunming Institute of Botany, pers. comm.

4 Ibid.

5 Li-Jun Yan, Kunming Institute of Botany, pers. comm.

6 'Nu Ethnic Minority', www.chinatravel.com, accessed 23 December 2015.

7 Dr Mao Kangshan, Sichuan University, Chengdu, pers. comm.

8 Ibid.

9 Li-Jun Yan, Kunming Institute of Botany, pers. comm.

10 Terry Kleeman, *Great Perfection* (Honolulu, HI, 1998), p. 23; Dr Wu Zengyuan, Kunming Institute of Botany, pers. comm.

11 Guomei, *Rhododendrons of China*, vol. 1, p. 4.

12 'buru guiqi' in Chinese; C. T. Hsia et al., eds, *The Columbia Anthology of Yuan Drama* (New York, 2014), note 103, p. 368.

13 Kleeman, *Great Perfection*, p. 23.

14 Jessica Yeung, *Ink Dances in Limbo: Gao Xingjian's Writing as Cultural Translation* (Hong Kong, 2008), p. 112; Hsia et al., *The Columbia Anthology of Yuan Drama*, p. 304.

15 Elizabeth Georgian, pers. comm.

16 Dr Mao Kangshan, Sichuan University, Chengdu, pers. comm.

17 Ibid.
18 William M. Simmons, 'The Mystic Voice: Pequot Folklore from the Seventeenth Century to the Present', in *The Pequots in Southern New England: The Fall and Rise of an American Indian Nation*, ed. Laurence Hauptman and James Wherry (Norman, OK, 1993), p. 151; Bill Anthes, 'Indian Time at Foxwoods', in *(Im)permanence: Cultures In/Out of Time*, ed. Judith Schachter and Stephen Brockmann (Pittsburg, PA, 2008), pp. 237–47.
19 Bill Anthes, 'Learning from Foxwoods; Visualizing the Mashantucket Pequot Tribal Nation', *American Indian Quarterly*, XXXII (2008), pp. 204–18.
20 Narayan Mahanandar, *Plants and People of Nepal* (Portland, OR, 2002), p. 58.
21 Daphne du Maurier, *Rebecca*, 1980 edn (London, 1980), p. 6.
22 Ibid., p. 70.
23 Ibid., pp. 88–9.
24 Ibid., p. 114.
25 Ibid., pp. 132, 174 and 287.
26 Sylvia Plath, *Collected Poems*, ed. Ted Hughes (London, 1981); also see J. M. Bremer, 'Three Approaches to Sylvia Plath's "Electra on Azalea Path"', *Neophilogus*, LXXVI (1992), pp. 305–16.
27 Sylvia Plath, *Collected Poems*; and see 'When Otto Plath died in 1940, Sylvia and her brother Warren didn't attend his funeral', www.lovingsylvia. tumblr.com, accessed 19 September 2015.
28 Harriet Staff, 'Newly Released FBI Files Corroborate Sylvia Plath's Characterization of Her Father as Pro-Nazi', www.poetryfoundation.org, 20 August 2012.
29 Plath, *Collected Poems*.
30 Jack Wernick, 'Azalea Path', www.jackwernick.weebly.com, accessed 11 August 2016.
31 Tim Bowling, *The Thin Smoke of the Heart* (Montreal and Ithaca, NY, 2000), p. 14.
32 Colin Smith, 'Launch of Azalea Dreams, Bamboo Lives by Wee Kiat', www.youtube.com, 8 November 2013.
33 Yaba Badoe, *True Murder* (London, 2009), p. 20.
34 Pete Hautman and Mary Logue, *The Bloodwater Mysteries: Doppelganger* (New York, 2008), p. 20.
35 Jeanine Larmoth and Charlotte Snyder Turgeon, *Murder on the Menu* (New York, 1972), p. 43.
36 Rosella Rhine, *Murder by Wheelchair* (ebook, 2014), p. 4.
37 'Schedule 9 of the Wildlife and Countryside Act 1981', www.ukwildlife.com, accessed 19 September 2015.
38 Jan Bondeson, *Murder Houses of London* (Stroud, 2014); Thomas Jacobs, *Pageant of Murder* (London, 1956), pp. 47–9.
39 Dr David Chamberlain, pers. comm.
40 Frances Brody, *Murder on a Summer's Day* (London, 2013); Penny de Byl, *Lost Souls* (Dartford, 2014), pp. 165 and 181.

8 Black Sheep: The Tale of *Rhododendron ponticum*

1 At co-ordinates 52°14′58″N, 7°57′53″W.

2 Rachel Flaherty, 'Rhododendron Rescue: Walkers Trapped by Plants for Five Hours', www.irishtimes.com, 17 June 2014; 'Hillwalkers Trapped for Five Hours in Rhododendron Plants', www.rte.ie, 17 June 2014.

3 Clive Stace, *New Flora of the British Isles*, 3rd edn (Cambridge, 2010), p. 526; 'Schedule 9 of the Wildlife and Countryside Act 1981', www.ukwildlife.com, accessed 19 September 2015.

4 K. Dehnen-Schmutz and M. Williamson, '*Rhododendron ponticum* in Britain and Ireland: Social, Economic and Ecological Factors in its Successful Invasion', *Environment and History*, XII (2006), pp. 325–50; G. Doyle, 'Laurophyllisation in Ireland – The Case of *Rhododendron ponticum*', in *Conference on Recent Shifts in Vegetation Boundaries of Deciduous Forests, Especially due to General Global Warming*, ed. F. Klotzli and G. R. Walther (Basel, 1999), pp. 237–51.

5 Doyle, 'Laurophyllisation in Ireland – the Case of *Rhododendron ponticum*'; J. R. Cross, 'Biological Flora of the British Isles: *Rhododendron ponticum* L.', *Journal of Ecology*, LXIII (1975), pp. 345–64; R. H. Gritten, '*Rhododendron ponticum* and Some Other Invasive Plants in the Snowdonia National Park', in *Plant Invasions: General Aspects and Special Problems. Workshop Held at Kostelec nad Černými Lesy, Czech Republic* (1993), pp. 213–19.

6 A. P. Colak et al., '*Rhododendron ponticum* in Native and Exotic Environments, with Particular Reference to Turkey and the British Isles', *Journal of Practical Ecology and Conservation*, II (1998), pp. 34–41.

7 C. M. Stephenson et al., 'Modelling Establishment Probabilities of an Exotic Plant, *Rhododendron ponticum*, Invading a Heterogeneous, Woodland Landscape using Logistic Regression with Spatial Autocorrelation', *Ecological Modelling*, CXCIII (2006), pp. 747–58; J.M.B. Brown, 'The *Rhododendron* Problem in the Woodlands of Southern England', *Quarterly Journal of Forestry*, XLVII (1953), pp. 239–53; J.M.B. Brown, '*Rhododendron ponticum* in British Woodlands', in *Report on Forestry Reserves 1953* (London, 1954), pp. 42–3.

8 P. Simons, 'The Day of the Rhododendron', *New Scientist*, CXIX (1988), pp. 50–54; and for example see 'Rhododendron Burning at Muiravonside Country Park', http://blogs.tcv.org.uk, 11 September 2015.

9 Cross, 'Biological Flora of the British Isles: *Rhododendron ponticum* L.'; D. F. Chamberlain, 'A Revision of *Rhododendron*. II. Subgenus *Hymenanthes*', *Notes from the Royal Botanic Garden Edinburgh*, XXXIX (1982), p. 313.

10 R. I. Milne and R. J. Abbott, 'Origin and Evolution of Invasive Naturalized Material of *Rhododendron ponticum* L. in the British Isles', *Molecular Ecology*, V (2000), pp. 541–56.

11 K. Jessen, '*Rhododendron ponticum* in the Irish Interglacial Flora', *Irish Naturalists' Journal*, IX (1948), pp. 174–5; K. Jessen et al., 'The Interglacial Flora', *Proceedings of the Royal Irish Academy*, LXB (1959), pp. 1–77; Harry Godwin, *History of the British Flora* (Cambridge, 1975), pp. 292–3; Martin

Ingrouille, *Historical Ecology of the British Flora* (London and New York, 2012), p. 82.

12 S. Campbell et al., *Quaternary of Southwest England* (London, 1998), pp. 149–50.

13 Jessen, '*Rhododendron ponticum* in the Irish Interglacial Flora'; Jessen et al., 'The Interglacial Flora'; Godwin, *History of the British Flora*, pp. 292–3; Ingrouille, *Historical Ecology of the British Flora*, p. 82.

14 Stace, *New Flora of the British Isles*, pp. 524–30; Tim Robinson, *Connemara: Listening to the Wind* (Dublin, 2007).

15 Robinson, *Connemara*, pp. 39–42.

16 D. L. Kelly, 'The Native Forest Vegetation of Killarney, South-west Ireland: An Ecological Account', *Journal of Ecology*, LXIX (1981), pp. 437–72.

17 M. S. Skeffington, 'Ireland's Lusitanian Heathers – An *Erica mackayana* Perspective', *Ecological Questions*, XXI (2015), pp. 13–15.

18 '*Rhododendron ponticum* (rhododendron)', www.cabi.org, accessed 19 September 2015.

19 Alice Coats, *Garden Shrubs and Their Histories* (London, 1963).

20 Milne and Abbott, 'Origin and Evolution of Invasive Naturalized Material of *Rhododendron ponticum*'.

21 Doyle, 'Laurophyllisation in Ireland – The Case of *Rhododendron ponticum*'.

22 W. Curtis, '*Rhododendron ponticum*', *Botanical Magazine*, XVI (1803), p. 650.

23 P. Frost, 'Rhododendrons', *The Gardeners' Chronicle* (1841), p. 85.

24 J. Rinz, 'Remark on Various Gardens about London, and in Other Parts of England, Visited in April and May 1829', *Gardener's Magazine* (1829), p. 382.

25 Dehnen-Schmutz and Williamson, '*Rhododendron ponticum* in Britain and Ireland'. Prices are all converted to 2002 GB pounds.

26 S. C. Michalak, '*Rhododendron ponticum*', DHE thesis, Royal Botanic Gardens, Edinburgh, 1976.

27 Dehnen-Schmutz and Williamson, '*Rhododendron ponticum* in Britain and Ireland'.

28 Michalak, '*Rhododendron ponticum*'.

29 W. Craw, 'Rhododendrons as cover for game', *The Gardeners' Chronicle and Agricultural Gazette* (1864), p. 54.

30 W. Goldring, 'Rhododendrons Versus Laurel', *The Garden* (1864), p. 280.

31 Dehnen-Schmutz and Williamson, '*Rhododendron ponticum* in Britain and Ireland'.

32 G. Wythes, 'The Common Rhododendron in Woods and Drives', *The Garden* (January–June 1891), p. 424; Arthur Osborn, *Shrubs and Trees for the Garden* (London, 1933).

33 A. D. Webster, 'Game Coverts', *The Gardeners' Chronicle* (1883), p. 792.

34 By comparison, the mean February temperature for 1931–60 was +3.9°C: G. Manley, 'Central England Temperatures: Monthly Means 1659 to 1973', *Quarterly Journal of the Royal Meteorological Society*, C (1974), pp. 389–405.

35 Anon., 'The Frost of 1895', *British Medical Journal*, I (20 April 1895), p. 886; Anon., 'CCCCXCV – The Great Frost of 1895', *Bulletin of*

Miscellaneous Information (Royal Botanic Gardens, Kew), MDCCCXCVI (1896), pp. 5–10.

36 Field, 'The Pontic Rhododendrons and the Frost', *The Garden* (20 April 1895), p. 270.

37 C. L. Justice, 'The Victorian Rhododendron Story', *Journal of the American Rhododendron Society*, LIII/3 (1999); J. G. Millais, *Rhododendrons and the Various Hybrids* (London, 1917), facing p. 12.

38 E. A. Rübel, 'The International Phytogeographical Excursion in the British Isles. V. The Killarney Woods', *New Phytologist*, XI (1912), pp. 54–7; Bean, *Trees and Shrubs Hardy in the British Isles*, p. 372.

39 Michalak, '*Rhododendron ponticum*'.

40 Frederick Street, *Hardy Rhododendrons* (London, 1954), p. 132.

41 E.H.M. Cox and P. A. Cox, *Modern Rhododendrons* (London, 1956), p. 24.

42 G. Bell, 'Halfdan Lem, Hybridizer', *Journal of the American Rhododendron Society*, XXXI/1 (1977).

43 'HL Deb 06 June 1986 vol 475 cc1243–70', http://hansard. millbanksystems.com, 6 June 1986; 'HC Deb 04 May 2000 vol 349 cc302–86', http://hansard.millbanksystems.com, 4 May 2000. The TV reference was on *Daily Politics*.

44 Osborn, *Shrubs and Trees for the Garden*.

45 Dehnen-Schmutz and Williamson, '*Rhododendron ponticum* in Britain and Ireland'.

46 May Cowan, *Inverewe: A Garden in the North-west Highlands* (London, 1964), p. 117.

47 Maggie Campbell-Culver, *The Origin of Plants: The People and Plants that have Shaped Britain's Garden History Since the Year 1000* (London, 2001), pp. 235–8.

48 Jack Cant, 'Killer Plants Stalk Queen Mum', in *The Best of the Sunday Sport* (London, 1989), p. 42.

49 See Lanning Roper, *The Gardens in the Royal Park at Windsor* (London, 1959).

50 Colak et al., '*Rhododendron ponticum* in Native and Exotic Environments'.

51 Dehnen-Schmutz and Williamson, '*Rhododendron ponticum* in Britain and Ireland'.

52 J. R. Cross, 'The Establishment of *Rhododendron ponticum* in the Killarney Oakwoods, s.w. Ireland', *Journal of Ecology*, LXIX (1981), pp. 807–24; Stephenson et al., 'Modelling Establishment Probabilities of an Exotic Plant'.

53 Milne and Abbott, 'Origin and Evolution of Invasive Naturalized Material of *Rhododendron ponticum*'.

54 Field, 'The Pontic Rhododendrons and the Frost'.

55 E. T. Nilsen, 'The Relationship Between Freezing Tolerance and Thermotropic Leaf Movement in Five *Rhododendron* Species', *Oecologia*, LXXXVII (1991), pp. 63–71.

56 Dehnen-Schmutz and Williamson, '*Rhododendron ponticum* in Britain and Ireland'.

57 J. Cullen, 'Naturalised Rhododendrons Widespread in Great Britain and Ireland', *Hanburyana*, V (2011), pp. 11–19.

58 Kenneth Cox, 'Why So Called "*R.* x *superponticum*" is Invalid Taxonomy and Has No Scientific Basis', www.glendoick.com, 1 January 2014.

59 Cross, 'The Establishment of *Rhododendron ponticum* in the Killarney Oakwoods, s.w. Ireland'; Colak et al., '*Rhododendron ponticum* in Native and Exotic Environments'.

60 Colak et al., '*Rhododendron ponticum* in Native and Exotic Environments'; A. C. Dietzsch et al., 'Relative Abundance of an Invasive Alien Plant Affects Native Pollination Processes', *Oecologia*, CLXVII (2011), pp. 469– 79; Cross, 'Biological Flora of the British Isles: *Rhododendron ponticum* L.'; C. A. Sutton and D. M. Wilkinson, 'The Effects of *Rhododendron* on Testate Amoebae Communities in Woodland Soils in North West England', *Acta Protozoologica*, XLVI (2007), pp. 333–8.

61 I. D. Rotherham and D. J. Read, 'Aspects of the Ecology of *Rhododendron ponticum* with Reference to its Competitive and Invasive Properties', *Aspects of Applied Biology*, XVI (1988), pp. 327–35; Benjamin Davis, 'The Mechanisms Used by the Invasive Shrub *Rhododendron ponticum* to Inhibit the Growth of Surrounding Vegetation', PhD thesis, University of Southampton, 2013; James Merryweather, '*Rhododendron* Poisons the Soil, Doesn't It? Chinese Whispers Become Conservation Lore', www.slef.org.uk, accessed 19 September 2015.

62 Angelo Salsi, 'Alien Species and Nature Conservation in the EU. The Role of the LIFE Program', www.ec.europa.eu, 2004; R. J. Mitchell et al., 'A Comparative Study of the Seedbanks of Heathland and Successional Habitats in Dorset, Southern England', *Journal of Ecology*, LXXXVI (1998), pp. 588–96; Deborah Long and Jill Williams, '*Rhododendron ponticum*: Impact on Lower Plants and Fungi Communities on the West Coast of Scotland', www.plantlife.org, November 2007, p. 39.

63 '*Rhododendron ponticum* (rhododendron)', www.cabi.org.

64 'Rhododendron control', http://forestry.gov.uk, accessed 19 September 2015.

65 'History of the Isabella Plantation', www.royalparks.org.uk, accessed 19 September 2015; 'Windsor Great Park Berkshire/Surrey', www.countryfile.com, accessed 19 September 2015; also personal observations by author.

66 Marianne Elliott, 'Life Cycle of *Phytophthora ramorum* as it Relates to Soil and Water', www.forestphytophthoras.org, accessed 19 September 2015.

67 '*Phytophthora ramorum* and *P. kernoviae*', www.rhs.org.uk, accessed 19 September 2015.

68 'Rhododendron', www.eryri-npa.gov.uk, accessed 19 September 2015; 'Observations of *Rhododendron* in Killarney Oakwood Areas Cleared & Maintained by Groundwork Conservation Volunteers in the Period 1981–2015', www.groundwork.ie, 14 June 2014; Kevin Hughes, 'Rhododendron Issue Sparks War of Words', www.independent.ie, 31 January 2015.

69 'Rhododendron', www.eryri-npa.gov.uk; '*Rhododendron ponticum* (rhododendron)', www.cabi.org; Gritten, '*Rhododendron ponticum* and some other Invasive Plants in the Snowdonia National Park'.

70 'Rhododendron Control', http://forestry.gov.uk; Colin Edwards and Sarah Taylor, 'A Survey and Strategic Appraisal of Rhododendron Invasion and Control in Woodland Areas in Argyll and Bute', http://forestry.gov.uk, June 2008.

71 L. C. Foxcroft et al., *Plant Invasions in Protected Areas: Patterns, Problems and Challenges* (New York, 2013), pp. 229–30; Angelo Salsi, 'Alien Species and Nature Conservation in the EU. The Role of the LIFE Program', www.ec.europa.eu.

72 A. Bremner and K. Park, 'Public Attitudes to the Management of Invasive Non-native Species in Scotland', *Biological Conservation*, CXXXIX (2007), pp. 306–14; additional data from this study shared with author.

73 Personal comments made to the author; I. D. Rotherham, *The Wild Rhododendron* (Sheffield, 2004).

74 Colak et al., '*Rhododendron ponticum* in Native and Exotic Environments'.

75 Anon., 'Whitley Park', *Huddersfield District Chronicle* (18 April 1997).

76 'HC Deb 11 June 1997 vol 295 cc1116–25', http://hansard.millbanksystems.com, 11 June 1997.

77 Ibid.

78 Colak et al., '*Rhododendron ponticum* in Native and Exotic Environments'.

79 George Monbiot, 'Sheepwrecked', www.monbiot.com, 30 May 2013.

80 Jenny Wong et al., *Report of the Rhododendron Feasibility Study. Prepared for the Beddgelert Rhododendron Management Group by the School of Agricultural and Forest Sciences* (Bangor, 2002), pp. 2–3.

81 'Invasive Plant Legislation', www.glendoick.com, accessed 19 September 2015; go to http://bsbi.org/maps and type 'Rhododendron' to see all species and cultivars recorded wild from Britain.

82 Beverley Knowles, 'The Vicar's Got a Puncture', http://beverleyknowles.com, accessed 19 September 2015.

83 Nathalie Levi, '"Bad Artists Copy, Good Artists Steal." [1], What's Yours is Mine, Roisin Byrne & Duncan Wooldridge at Tenderpixel', https://nathalielevi.wordpress.com, accessed 24 January 2017.

9 Conservation, Collections and the Future

1 Pradeep Kumar, 'Assessment of Impact of Climate Change on Rhododendrons in Sikkim Himalayas using Maxent Modelling: Limitations and Challenges', *Biodiversity and Conservation*, XXI (2012), pp. 1251–66.

2 'Corrour Lodge, Fort William, Scotland', www.parksandgardens.org, 25 May 2014; Brenda McLean, *George Forrest, Plant Hunter* (Woodbridge, 2004), p. 133.

3 'Rhododendron Species Conservation Group', www.rscg.org.uk.

4 'Glendoick', www.glendoick.com, accessed 19 September 2015; 'Scotland Inverewe Garden: A Surprising Tropical Paradise', www.insiders-scotland-guide.com, accessed 24 January 2017.

5   Francis Kingdon-Ward, *Himalayan Enchantment: An Anthology* (London, 1990), p. 130.

6   Euan Cox, *Plant Hunting in China* (London, 1945), p. 208; Narayan Mahanandar, *Plants and People of Nepal* (Portland, OR, 2002), p. 24.

7   K. K. Singh et al., 'Rhododendrons Conservation in the Sikkim Himalaya', *Current Science*, LXXXV (2003), pp. 602–6.

8   Francis Kingdon-Ward et al., *Frank Kingdon Ward's Riddle of the Tsangpo Gorges: Retracing the Epic Journey of 1924–25 in South-east Tibet*, 2nd edn (Woodbridge, 2008).

9   Prem Shankar Jha, 'Why India and China Should Leave the Yarlung Tsangpo Alone', www.chinadialogue.net, 5 March 2014; Archana Chaudhary, 'India Plans Dam on Tsangpo-Brahmaputra to Check Floods and China', www.bloomberg.com, 4 June 2015.

10 Y. Lü et al. 'A Policy-driven Large Scale Ecological Restoration: Quantifying Ecosystem Services Changes in the Loess Plateau of China', *PLOS ONE*, VII (2012): e31782.

11 Y. P. Ma et al., 'A New Species of *Rhododendron* (Ericaceae) from Baili Rhododendron Nature Reserve, NW Guizhou, China', *Phytotaxa*, CXCV (2015), pp. 197–200.

12 '*Flora of China*', www.efloras.org, vol. XVIII, p. 239, accessed 19 September 2015.

13 A. P. Colak et al., '*Rhododendron ponticum* in Native and Exotic Environments, with Particular Reference to Turkey and the British Isles', *Journal of Practical Ecology and Conservation*, II (1998), pp. 34–41.

14 Seen by the author, and Dr Maria Chamberlain.

15 Toby Musgrave et al., *The Plant Hunters* (London, 1999), p. 170.

16 Dr David Chamberlain, pers. comm.

17 Douglas Gibbs et al., *The Red List of Rhododendrons* (Richmond, 2011).

18 'Royal Botanic Garden, Edinburgh', www.rbge.org.uk, accessed 19 September 2015.

19 Singh et al., 'Rhododendrons Conservation in the Sikkim Himalaya'; O. N. Tiwari and U. K. Chauhan, 'Rhododendron Conservation in Sikkim Himalaya', *Current Science*, XC (2006), pp. 532–41.

20 Alleyne Cook, 'Tower Court: A Personal Account – Part II', *Journal of the American Rhododendron Society*, LI/3 (1997).

21 Lanning Roper, *The Gardens in the Royal Park at Windsor* (London, 1959), pp. 96–7, 103.

22 Cox, *Plant Hunting in China*, p. 177.

23 Kingdon-Ward et al., *Frank Kingdon Ward's Riddle of the Tsangpo Gorges*.

24 Archie Skinner, 'Rescuing the Ghent and Rustica Flore Pleno Azaleas', *Journal of the American Rhododendron Society*, XXXVIII/3 (1984).

25 Frederick Street, *Hardy Rhododendrons* (London, 1954), p. 17.

26 G. H. Pinckney, 'The Knap Hill and Exbury Strain of Azaleas', *Journal of the American Rhododendron Society*, VII/1 (1953).

27 Dr Wu Zengyuan, Kunming Institute of Botany, pers. comm.

28 Cox, *Plant Hunting in China*, p. 211.

29 K. S. Gaira et al., 'Impact of Climate Change on the Flowering of *Rhododendron arboreum* in Central Himalaya, India', *Current Science*, CVI (2014), pp. 1735–8; Hari Kumar Shrestha, 'Climate Change Threatening Rhododendron', www.nepalmountainnews.com, 17 March 2015.

30 Kumar, 'Assessment of Impact of Climate Change on Rhododendrons in Sikkim Himalayas'; Pradeep Kumar, 'Biogeographic Response of *Rhododendron* to Climate Change in the Sikkim Himalaya', www.sikkimforest.gov.in, accessed 19 September 2015.

31 Street, *Hardy Rhododendrons*, p. 132.

32 G. Donald Waterer, 'Rhododendrons and Azaleas at the Knap Hill Nursery', *Journal of the American Rhododendron Society*, IV/1 (1950).

33 IPCC, 'Summary for Policy Makers', in *Climate Change 2014: Impacts, Adaptation, and Vulnerability. Part A: Global and Sectoral Aspects. Contribution of Working Group II to the Fifth Assessment Report of the Intergovernmental Panel on Climate Change*, ed. C. B. Field et al. (Cambridge and New York, 2014), pp. 1–32.

Further Reading

Briggs, Roy, 'Chinese' Wilson: A Life of Ernest H. Wilson, 1876–1930 (London, 1993)

Brown, Jane, Tales of the Rose Tree (London, 2004)

Coats, Alice, The Quest for Plants (London, 1969)

Desmond, Ray, Sir Joseph Dalton Hooker, Traveller and Plant Collector (Woodbridge, 1998)

du Maurier, Daphne, Rebecca (London, 1980)

Fforde, Jasper, Shades of Grey (London, 2011)

Halliday, Pat, The Illustrated Rhododendron: Their Classification Portrayed Through the Artwork of Curtis's Botanical Magazine (London, 2001)

Kingdon-Ward, Francis, Himalayan Enchantment: An Anthology (London, 1990)

— et al., Frank Kingdon Ward's Riddle of the Tsangpo Gorges: Retracing the Epic Journey of 1924–25 in South-East Tibet, 2nd edn (Woodbridge, 2008)

McLean, Brenda, George Forrest: Plant Hunter (Woodbridge, 2004)

Mueggler, Erik, The Paper Road: Archive and Experience in the Botanical Exploration of West China and Tibet (Berkeley, CA, and London, 2011)

Musgrave, Toby et al., The Plant Hunters (London, 1999)

O'Brien, Seamus, In the Footsteps of Augustine Henry (Woodbridge, 2011)

Roper, Lanning, The Gardens in the Royal Park at Windsor (London, 1959)

Rose, Sarah, For All the Tea in China: Espionage, Empire and the Secret Formula for the World's Favourite Drink (London, 2013)

Shephard, Sue, Seeds of Fortune: A Gardening Dynasty (London, 2003)

Associations and Websites

THE AMERICAN RHODODENDRON SOCIETY
www.rhododendron.org

AZALEA SOCIETY OF AMERICA
www.azaleas.org

EDINBURGH RHODODENDRON MONOGRAPHS
http://data.rbge.org.uk/service/factsheets/Edinburgh_Rhododendron_
Monographs.xhtml

HENNING'S RHODODENDRON & AZALEA PAGES
www.rhodyman.net/rhodyn.php

HIRSUTUM.INFO: ABOUT RHODODENDRONS, AZALEAS AND VIREYAS;
A VIRTUAL ARBORETUM
www.hirsutum.info

JOURNAL OF THE AMERICAN RHODODENDRON SOCIETY:
DIGITAL ARCHIVE
http://scholar.lib.vt.edu/ejournals/JARS

NEW ZEALAND RHODODENDRON ASSOCIATION
www.rhododendron.org.nz

RHODODENDRON SPECIES CONSERVATION GROUP
www.rscg.org.uk

THE RHS RHODODENDRON, CAMELLIA & MAGNOLIA GROUP
www.rhodogroup-rhs.org

THE SCOTTISH RHODODENDRON SOCIETY
www.scottishrhododendronsociety.org.uk

VIREYA RHODODENDRONS
www.vireya.net

Acknowledgements

In writing this book I have depended greatly on the magnificent resource that is the library of the Royal Botanic Garden, Edinburgh, so thanks are due to all those involved in creating and maintaining this library. The rhododendron photos taken for this book are from the living collections of the Royal Botanic Gardens of Edinburgh and Kew, The Valley Gardens at Windsor Great Park, Wisley Gardens, the Sir Harold Hillier Gardens, Isabella Plantation in Richmond Park, The Lost Gardens of Heligan, and Trebah in Cornwall. Particular thanks are due to Louise Galloway at Edinburgh, and the warden at Isabella Plantation, for access to private nursery collections.

Invaluable assistance in viewing Veitch Nurseries catalogues was provided by the RHS reference collection. For other images, including some I requested but did not use, thanks are due to Jim Barlup, Drs David and Maria Chamberlain, Everard Daniel, Janet and Adrian Dyer, Dr Richard Ennos, John Foley, Dr Anil Joshi, Tadeusz Kusibab, Liu Jie, Emma Mather-Pike, Andrew Milne, David Purvis, Dr Salih Terzioğlu, Jack Wernick, Wu Zengyuan, the Bridgwater Museum, the Carey Centre, the Edinburgh Forrest Archive, the Getty Museum, Hackney Museum, HESCO, Portland Chapter of the Rhododendron Society, the Royal Horticultural Society, the Royal Irish Academy, Select Books, SEMRA, the *Sunday Sport*, and the Wilson Archive at Harvard.

Chinese folk tales were told to the author by Dr Mao Kangshan, Dr Wu Zengyuan and Yan Li-Jun, while an Estonian incident was described by Georgi and Nelli Viktorov. Invaluable advice and information were provided to the author by Dr Alison Bremner, Drs David and Maria Chamberlain, Dr Kate Creasey, Ryan Douglas, Dr Gao Lianming, Elizabeth Georgian, Ian Hedge, Dr Ma Yongpeng, Dr Monique Simmonds, James Stephens at Heligan, and Dr Rebecca Yahr.

Lastly, and perhaps most importantly, this book could not have been written without the love and support of my wife Nenya Viktorova Milne, and childcare assistance (and soup) from her mother Nelli Viktorova.

Photo Acknowledgements

The author and publishers wish to express their thanks to the below sources of illustrative material and/or permission to reproduce it. All photos not listed below were taken by the author.

Richard Ennos, Anton Hardinger via Aroche on Wikimedia, SB Johnny on Wikimedia: p. 35, top row, left to right (bottom row taken by author); Drawn by author, from data supplied by Dr Alison Bremner: p. 66; Bridgwater Museum: p. 72 middle image (others by author); images made available by Andrew Butko via Wikimedia: p. 12; Courtesy of Center for Study of the Life and Work of William Carey, D. D. (1761–1834), William Figure drawn by author using own photos plus photos taken by Jim Barlup (White Ginger), Everard Daniel (Gomer Waterer), Miranda Gun (Mrs Lindsay Smith), Tadeusz Kusibab (Madame Carvalho), and the Portland Chapter of the Rhododendron Society (Trude Webster): p. 66; Carey University, Hattiesburg, Mississippi, USA: p. 54; Dr David Chamberlain: p. 140; Dr Maria Chamberlain: p. 119; Painting by Janet Dyer: p. 160; John Foley and SEMRA: pp. 155, 170; Glass plate negatives 1/4 ET 14 for the collectors and 5/4 L 9 from the Forrest archive, Royal Botanic Garden, Edinburgh: pp. 100, 102; Digital image courtesy of the Getty's Open Content Program: p. 73; Photo by Ernest Wilson, courtesy of Arnold Arboretum Horticultural Library of Harvard University: © President and Fellows of Harvard College, Arnold Arboretum Archives: p. 97; Makers of British Botany via Hesperian on Wikimedia: p. 53; Images taken from K. Jessen et al., 'The Interglacial Flora', *Proceedings of the Royal Irish Academy*, LXB (1959), plate II: p. 157; Photo courtesy of Liu Jie and Wu Zengyuan: p. 14 (top); Photo courtesy of Dr Anil Joshi and HESCO: p. 121; Emma Mather-Pike: p. 131; Courtesy of the Royal Horticultural Society, Lindley Library, with colours added by author: p. 84; Courtesy of the Royal Horticultural Society, Lindley Library: p. 87; Courtesy of *The Sunday Sport*: p. 164; Dr Salih Terzioğlu: p. 117; Victoria and Albert Museum, London: p. 150; Image conceived by Jack Wernick, and created by Jack Wernick and Hal-JannenDesign, featuring Hannah Daisy Brandt and Emily Ciotti, © Jack Wernick: p. 146; Image made available by World Imaging via Wikimedia; (Pompey): p. 116.

Index